SO YOU THINK
YOU KNOW THE

Clive Gifford

**The Old Aerodrome,
Beccles, NR34 7SP**

www.tobar.co.uk

We would like to thank the following people for their contribution of ideas to this book:
Elspeth Henderson, Emily Thomas, Emma Layfield, James Atkin, Jenny Dalglish, Kirsty Hamilton, Leilani Sparrow, Rachel Mynott and Venetia Gosling.

© Hodder Children's Books 2004

First published in Great Britain in 2004 by Hodder Children's Books

This edition exclusively published for Tobar 2008 www.tobar.co.uk

Editor: Hayley Leach
Design by Fiona Webb
Cover design: Hodder Children's Books

The right of Clive Gifford to be identified as the author of the work has been asserted by him in accordance with the Copyright, Designs and Patents Act 1988.

ISBN: 978 0 340 98830 5

Printed in the UK by CPI Bookmarque, Croydon, CR0 4TD

The paper and board used in this paperback by Hodder Children's Books are natural recyclable products made from wood grown in sustainable forests. The manufacturing processes conform to the environmental regulations of the country of origin.

Hodder Children's Books
a division of Hachette Children's Books
338 Euston Road, London NW1 3BH
An Hachette Livre UK company

CONTENTS

INTRODUCTION

So you think you know all about the eighties? Think you can recall all the fun and fashions, fads, foods and films of the decade? Let us take you back to a time of Sinclair Spectrums, the SDP and *SuperTed*, when the pound in your pocket was made of paper and the World Wide Web was just a glint in the eye of a few visionaries. In this book, you will find over 1,000 questions covering many aspects of life in the eighties from Madonna to *Masters of the Universe*, from rap to Roland Rat and from Delorean to *Dynasty*. Whether you were into the *Breakfast Club* or the Hacienda Club, break dancing or *Dirty Dancing*, power suits or shell suits, we hope there's something in this book which triggers some happy memories.

Biography

Clive Gifford is an award-winning writer and journalist with over 50 books published, including *Eyewitness Guide: Media, The Kingfisher Geography Encyclopaedia* and *The Water Puppets*, a children's novel set during the Vietnam War.

As a teenager, Clive lived out the eighties dream of glamour (he owned a pair of moon boots and a pair of Levi 501s), media celebrity (he reviewed the film *War Games* on *CBTV* and appeared on *GMTV*) and money. At age 17, he ran a computer games company, Mikroleisure, which in tune with the times, briefly boomed before busting. Still, it gave him enough dosh/wonga for a Mini Metro, a Phillips Laserdisc and not one, but two ZX81 computers, both with 16K RAM packs. Now, that was flash.

In more recent times, Clive has contented himself with compiling more than a dozen quiz books on topics including the best-selling *So You Think You Know Harry Potter?*, *So You Think You Know David Beckham?* and *The Family Flip Quiz*, and he has worked as an editor on the *Who Wants to be a Millionaire?* quiz book.

KIDS' TELEVISION

1. Which cartoon superhero called Castle Grayskull his home?

2. If you were 'wide awake' in the eighties which bespectacled children's TV presenter were you watching?

3. Which Roland Rat sidekick was a leek-loving Welsh hamster?

4. Who was Dangermouse's permanently nervous ally?

5. What was the name of the Geordie boy *Grange Hill* hardgirl, Imelda Davies, had a vendetta against?

6. Sarah Greene, Keith Chegwin, Crow, and Sieve Head all appeared on which Saturday morning TV show?

7. Which cartoon show featured Autobots who fought the evil Decepticons?

8. Which show featured three choices of answer, with Mike 'Frank Butcher' Reid as the host?

9. Which long-running children's programme was hosted in the eighties by Stu Francis, and featured the Krankies and one of the first gunge tanks?

10. If you were watching Potsie and Ralph Malph make fools of themselves at Arnolds Drive-in, which show would you have been watching?

11. Who was Dangermouse's arch enemy?

12. In which children's puppet show of the 1980s did the *Porridge* prison warder, Mr Mckay, star?

13. Eric turned into which superhero in a 1983 cartoon show that featured the voices of *The Goodies*?

14. Which teacher versus pupil game show was hosted for a time by Bruno Brookes: *We are the Champions, Beat the Teacher* or *Screen Test*?

15. Which animated young children's show featured the Reverend Timms and handyman Ted Glenn?

16. Which show would you have been watching if you saw Danny Kendall reprimanded by Mrs McCluskey or Mr Bronson?

17. Which cartoon show featured six children transported into a realm of swords and sorcery where they were helped by a unicorn to fight the evil Venger?

18. Which young children's show featured Mr and Mrs Spoon, Eggbert and the Singing Hotpots?

19. Can you name the Radio One DJ who was the main host of *Saturday Superstore*?

20. What was the name of the gopher who featured on BBC children's TV?

21. What colour was Timmy Mallet's mallet?

22. Who was He-Man's avowed enemy?

23. Which children's show saw TV celebrities try to solve puzzles on the planet Arg and avoid falling into the Vortex?

24. Who was the key adversary of the Thundercats: Mumm-Ra, He-Hunter, Canosaur or Gargamel?

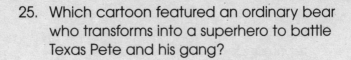

25. Which cartoon featured an ordinary bear who transforms into a superhero to battle Texas Pete and his gang?

26. Which fun action show featured four Vietnam veterans hired to help the innocent while on the run for a crime they didn't commit?

27. Kids' TV quiz show, *First Class*, featured a BBC Micro, Sinclair Spectrum or IBM PC called Eugene that kept the scores?

28. Which children's drama was set around a youth club in Newcastle?

29. What was the name of He-Man's faithful feline companion?

30. What was the name of the good-natured cartoon vet who travelled on a pogo stick?

31. Who was the leader of the Thundercats: Tygra, Lion-O, Panthro or Cheetara?

32. What was the name of Bill Cosby's character in the *Cosby Show*?

33. Zelda, Imperial Queen of Planet Guk, was the foe of the Transformers, Terrahawks, or Bananaman?

34. Which short animated show featured the antics in a creepy old castle of the characters Berk, Drutt and Boni – a skull's head?

35. If you heard someone say 'Whaddaya talkin' about Willis?' what show were you watching?

36. Which kids' drama showed Frazz, Spike, Tiddler, Lynda and others creating their school newspaper?

37. Which cartoon superhero's real identity was Princess Adora?

38. Latter-day *Austin Powers* star, Mike Myers, appeared on which children's TV show in the 1980s: *The Wide Awake Club*, *Saturday Banana*, *Magpie* or *Button Moon*?

39. Which canine cartoon version of *The Three Musketeers* appeared on our screens during the 1980s?

40. Donny Most, Ralph Malph from *Happy Days*, provided voices for *Dungeons and Dragons*, *He-Man* or *Bananaman*?

41. Chachi Arcola was the cousin of which character in *Happy Days*?

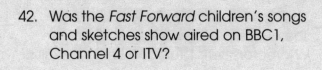

42. Was the *Fast Forward* children's songs and sketches show aired on BBC1, Channel 4 or ITV?

43. Azrael the cat wanted to eat which little blue cartoon creatures?

44. Which show did Tony Hart host for the first time in 1985: *Take Hart, Morph and Friends* or *Hartbeat*?

45. Dr Tiger Ninestein headed which cartoon group of futuristic earth defenders?

46. Which *Grange Hill* character's story was used as a vehicle for anti-drugs messages?

47. Who was the original host of *Pop Quiz*: Mike Read, Mike Smith or Gary Crowley?

48. What was the name of the postmistress in *Postman Pat*?

49. *Poparound* was a successor to *Runaround*, but which DJ did it feature in the place of Mike Reid?

50. What was the name of the character who led *The A-Team*?

CELEBRITIES

1. In which year did Prince Charles marry Lady Diana?

2. Who was shot and killed outside his New York apartment building on the 8th December 1980?

3. Which British actress, and star of *Dynasty*, appeared on the front cover of a 1983 edition of *Playboy*?

4. Which American comic and actor died of a drug overdose in March 1982?

5. Which Conservative minister resigned after admitting to being the father of a baby born to Sarah Keays?

6. How many children did Janet Walton give birth to in 1983?

7. Which member of the royal family was actually named Prince Henry Charles Albert David when he was born in 1984?

8. Which *Goon Show* star died in 1980?

9. Who did John W. Hinckley Jr try to assassinate in 1981?

10. Who became US President at the start of the 1980s?

11. Who did he beat in the 1980 US Presidential election?

12. What was the name of the child prodigy who received an Oxford University degree at the age of 13?

13. Which country did Ronald Reagan call the 'Evil Empire'?

14. What was the name of the man known as the Yorkshire Ripper?

15. In 1985, Kim Cotton became the UK's first: test tube baby, surrogate mother, female high court judge or first female general in the military forces?

16. Which European princess was killed in a car crash in 1983?

17. Menachem Begin was leader of which country prior to his retirement in 1983?

18. Which British journalist was kidnapped by Islamic Jihad in 1986?

19. Who resigned as deputy chairman of the Conservative Party in 1986: Michael Heseltine, Jeffrey Archer or Cecil Parkinson?

20. What was the name of the new member of the royal family born on the 21st June 1982?

21. Mother of ten, Victoria Gillick, became famous for protesting against what during the 1980s?

22. What was the name of the Buckingham Palace intruder who sat on the Queen's bed?

23. Who was Ronald Reagan's Vice President?

24. Which British novelist was the subject of a 'fatwah' prompted by the Iranian religious leader, Ayatollah Khomeni?

25. Which businessman broke the record for crossing the Atlantic in a boat in 1986?

26. Which South African civil rights activist was awarded the Nobel Peace Prize in 1984?

27. Queen Elizabeth's second son married in which year of the eighties?

28. Can you name two of the gang of four ex-Labour Party politicians who went on to form the SDP?

29. Which World War Two Nazi leader strangled himself in prison in 1987?

30. Can you name the madam who was acquitted of controlling prostitutes in 1987?

31. Which British political figure declared, 'This lady is not for turning', in the early 1980s?

32. What did the Dalai Lama win in 1989?

33. In which country was Paul McCartney arrested for possession of drugs in 1980?

34. Which religious figure became the first of his type to visit Britain for 450 years?

35. Dennis Nilsen was convicted in 1983 of murdering three, seven, nine or 17 men?

36. What did actor Rock Hudson die from in 1985?

37. On the 10th October 1985, Orson Wells and which famous bald-headed actor died?

38. How old was Lady Diana Spencer when she married Prince Charles?

39. Which chess grandmaster beat reigning champion Anatoly Karpov over a series of 48 matches in 1985?

40. Which member of the royal family attended the funeral of Japan's Emperor Hirihito in 1989?

41. Which Conservative junior health minister resigned in 1988 after a row over salmonella in eggs?

42. Who was elected mayor of the town of Carmel in California, in 1986?

43. Geraldine Ferraro became the first woman to run for President, Vice President or to run as a Supreme Court Judge for the US Democratic Party?

44. Which famous horse jockey was jailed for three years for tax evasion in 1987?

45. Michael Ryan gunned down and killed 14 people in 1987 in which South England town?

46. Benazir Bhutto became the leader of which Asian nation in 1988?

47. Which representative of the Archbishop of Canterbury was kidnapped in Beirut in 1987?

48. Which former leader of the Philippines died in 1989?

49. Which group won a Best New Artist Grammy in 1989, only to be stripped of the award when it was learned they were purely miming?

50. Who did Mark David Chapman kill?

FUN AND GAMES

1. How many 'pieces of pie' do you need to complete a Trivial Pursuit game?

2. Which doll turned 30 in 1989 and was sold in a special pink jubilee version?

3. Which three-speed boys' bike with a handlebar grip gear shift, replaced Raleigh's legendary Chopper?

4. Duplo bricks for very young children were launched by which toy company in 1983?

5. How many Teenage Mutant Ninja Turtles were there?

6. A Hungarian professor of architecture, with the first name Erno, invented what puzzle, which sold over 100 million in the early 1980s?

7. Which film prompted a range of action figures complete with a slime back pack?

8. If you were reading about a teenage boy and his love for Pandora Braithwaite, which book did you have in your hands?

9. What sort of creature was a Spit puppet?

10. Which computer suffered from 'RAM pack wobble' and came with just one kilobyte of memory?

11. What funny-faced dolls were originally called Little People before becoming top of many girls' Christmas lists from 1983 onwards?

12. Which company introduced its Burner range of BMX bikes in 1982 and, in under two years, had sold half a million of them?

13. 1983 saw the arrival of what sort of cuddly toy with a heart-shaped button as proof of authenticity?

14. What was the name of the brightly coloured disc surrounding a ball which kids could jump up and down on, a little like a pogo stick?

15. What changeable boy's figures, or cars, became Toy of the Year in 1985?

16. Which incredibly popular and addictive computer game was written by Russian Alexey Pazhitnov, in 1985?

17. What was the name of the computer game in which users had to navigate across a busy road?

18. What colour were the Art and Literature questions on a Trivial Pursuit board?

19. Which game, involving players drawing objects and phrases, was 1988 Game of the Year?

20. What popular eighties toy featured a toy kitchen sink, cooker and fold down table, all on two wheels so that it could be pulled around?

21. The computer game character, Mario, first appeared in: Donkey Kong Jr, Defender, Horace Goes Skiing or Ms Pacman?

22. Which popular 1980s doll travelled into space on board a 1985 space shuttle mission?

23. Blinky, Pinky, Inky and Clyde were four ghosts in which popular arcade game?

24. What colour was the case of the Sinclair ZX80 computer?

25. The Casio VL-Tone was an electronic guess-the-song game, a small portable music synthesizer or a very early digital camera?

26. Which horse-based toy came in many different colours with a mane you could comb and first arrived in Britain in 1983?

27. The Horace series of computer games were first found on the Sinclair Spectrum, the Commodore 64, the Dragon 32 or the BBC Model B?

28. Which collectable toy was around 5cm long and often came with a mini sleeping bag?

29. Can you name two of the Teenage Mutant Ninja Turtles that were a must-have toy in the late 1980s?

30. Optimus Prime and Megatron were He-Man figures, Thundercats figures, Transformers toys or Gobots?

31. Scalextric introduced a six lane race-track in 1987: true or false?

32. What was the name of the *Masters of the Universe* hero that was a popular action figure in the 1980s?

33. What was the name of the blond-haired American wrestler who became a popular boy's action figure in the mid-1980s?

34. How many squares were found on one face of a Rubik's Revenge puzzle, the successor to the Rubik's Cube?

35. What was the female Smurf character, available as both a toy and a pencil top, called?

36. What nautical brand of bubble bath came in a sailor-shaped bottle?

37. Which type of doll came with its own birth certificate and an individual name?

38. What was the collective name of the teddy bears that counted Love-a-Lot Bear, Grumpy Bear and Funshine Bear among their number?

39. Which company produced the Vic-20 and C64 home computers?

40. Which one of the following was not a new Subbuteo accessory in the 1980-1982 ranges: mounted police, simulated astro-turf pitch, crowd control barriers or long-haired footballers?

41. What handheld games computer was first introduced in Britain in 1989?

42. Which company produced football sticker albums, stickers for Disney collections and Barbie stickers?

43. Which popular British boys' toy ceased production in 1984: Raleigh Chopper, Action Man or Matchbox cars?

44. Jet Set Willy, Atic Atac and Knight Lore were all games available from which early 1980s home computer?

45. Subbuteo Hockey was introduced for girls in 1981: true or false?

46. Which game of moral dilemmas became available in Britain in the mid-1980s?

47. What colour was the History segment of the Trivial Pursuit game?

48. Which high-speed toy celebrated its thirtieth birthday in 1987?

49. Which of the following did the Raleigh Vektar bike, launched in 1985, not have: a FM radio on the handlebars, a *Star Wars* style design, retractable stabilizers or a built-in trip meter?

50. Butterscotch and Blossom were names of Cabbage Patch Kids, Beanie Babies or My Little Pony figures?

TELEVISION

1. What sitcom revolved around a bar where 'everybody knows your name'?

2. Which show featured Penelope Keith as Audrey fforbes-Hamilton?

3. The eighties started with the nation being gripped by the unmasking of which soap star's assailant?

4. Compo and Clegg were regulars in which comedy series?

5. What colour was the Trotter's van in *Only Fools and Horses*?

6. Which star of *Remington Steele* became a latter day James Bond?

7. Which alternative comedian played The Young Ones' landlord Jerzei Belowski?

8. Which comedy, set during the Korean War, finally bowed out in 1983 with a two and a half hour episode after 250, 30 minute shows?`

9. 'I Could be so Good for You' was the memorable theme tune of which comedy drama?

10. If you were watching a scruffy member of the lower classes reveal a 'cunning plan' to his master, what show would you have been viewing?

11. Which sitcom featured a wealthy American lady and her English butler: *Two's Company, You Say Potato* or *M'Lady and I*?

12. Which show were you watching if you saw a spaceship taken over by the powerful Despair Squid?

13. Captain Frank Furillo was in charge of a police force on which US show?

14. If you were watching the saga of the Colbys and the Carringtons, which show were you tuned into?

15. Who replaced Terry Wogan as the host of *Blankety Blank* in 1984?

16. In which show did Griff Rhys Jones play 'Bambi' Gascoigne, as Scumbag College fought Footlights, Oxbridge in a special edition of *University Challenge*?

17. What was the name of the detective agency in the show *Moonlighting*?

18. 'Now, that's magic!' was one of which diminutive magician's catchphrases?

19. Which American soap, a spin off from *Dynasty*, starred Charlton Heston and Stephanie Beacham?

20. Who was Sue-Ellen's brother in *Dallas*?

21. Which cerebral detective, based on the books of Colin Dexter, made his first TV appearance in 1987?

22. Which American private detective kept his gun in a coffee can and had a small printing press in his car?

23. Who were the first landlords of the Queen Vic in *EastEnders*?

24. What was the name of the character who was the resident head bartender at *Cheers*?

25. If you were watching Ford Prefect learning how to handle a Babel fish, what eighties TV show were you watching?

26. Which detective show featured a rich businessman and his journalist wife along with their chauffeur and general assistant, Max?

27. What was the occupation of the 1980 *Mastermind* champion, Fred Housego?

28. Which comedy drama show depicted a colourful group of bricklayers working on a site in Germany?

29. Which one of the following major movie stars did not make an appearance in *Miami Vice*: Wesley Snipes, Julia Roberts, Tom Cruise or Bruce Willis?

30. On which British channel did Max Headroom first appear?

31. Can you name Roseanne's two daughters?

32. In 1981, the fifty-second, and last, episode of which BBC sci-fi drama culminated in the death of most of the characters?

33. Which US action show featured Jan Michael Vincent as the pilot of an incredibly advanced military helicopter?

34. Which *Miami Vice* character was the tough cop from New York?

35. Was Edmund Blackadder a butler to the Prince Regent in the second, third or fourth *Blackadder* series?

36. Can you name the eighties show which was the first from the US to focus on two female police officers?

37. Which elderly female character was the star of *Murder She Wrote*, which first aired in 1985?

38. What show featured sketches about the racist policeman Constable Savage, Stout Life and a talking gorilla called Gerald?

39. Who did Blake Carrington marry in the first episode of *Dynasty*?

40. 'I am HAPPY' was the start of the theme tune to which ITV comedy of the early 1980s?

41. What was the name of the dog in *Hart to Hart*: Hightower, Freeway, Highway or Freeloader?

42. Who was the male bartender in *Cheers* before Woody's arrival?

43. Which *Only Fools and Horses* character had a wife called Marlene and always called Del, 'Derek'?

44. Which police drama focused on Jean Darblay who takes over a small Lancashire town's police station?

45. How many different actors portrayed Dr Who during the 1980s?

46. Who actually shot J.R. Ewing?

47. Which drama was based in the unlikely setting of a passenger ferry running between Amsterdam, Felixstowe and Stockholm?

48. What were the first names of the grandparents who lived with the Waltons?

49. Which show would you be watching if you saw a stuttering old storekeeper and his bumbling assistant, Granville?

50. What was the name of the character in the fourth series of *Blackadder*, played by the actor who had been Percy in series one and two?

MUSIC

1. How many red balloons did German singer, Nena, sing about?

2. What charity group's first single sold a staggering three and a half million copies?

3. Which German electronic band had a surprise number one hit in the eighties with 'The Model'?

4. *Three Feet High and Rising* was a hit album for which rap group?

5. Which band was fronted by a gold lame jacket-wearing Martin Fry?

6. Which songwriter and musician was a driving force in Depeche Mode, Yazoo and the Assembly during the 1980s?

7. With who did Cliff Richard re-record his sixties hit 'Living Doll'?

8. Can you name the lead singer of the Fine Young Cannibals?

9. Which hard rocking band had massive worldwide success with the 1983 album *Pyromania*?

10. 'Night Boat to Cairo', 'Baggy Trousers' and 'House of Fun' were all hits for which popular eighties band?

11. *But Seriously* was the third highest-selling album of the 1980s from which singer?

12. Which smooth female singer's album, *Diamond Life*, was a massive seller in the 1980s?

13. Which female singer had a major 1986 hit with 'So Macho'?

14. 'Happy Talk' was a novelty hit for which member of the Damned?

15. Which American outfit had a number one with the theme song from *Rocky III*?

16. In 1982, Soft Cell had their biggest hit. What was the song called?

17. Which Frankie Goes to Hollywood music video featured two world leaders fighting each other?

18. Aztec Camera, the Primitives or Orange Juice featured the songwriting talents of Roddy Frame?

19. What song, by the Matchroom Mob of snooker players and Chas 'n' Dave, was a surprise hit in 1986?

20. Harold Faltermeyer had 1985 chart success with 'Axel F', the theme tune to which movie?

21. Who fronted the Plastic Population and had a number one with 'The Only Way is Up'?

22. Which American artist had the biggest-selling album of the 1980s?

23. What was the name of the Human League's 1984 follow-up album to Dare?

24. Which rock band held the number one spot in the UK singles chart as the eighties began?

25. Which Beatles song was re-recorded under the title 'Ferry Aid' to assist the victims of the *Herald of Free Enterprise* ferry disaster?

26. Which Austrian-born singer had a number one hit with the single 'Rock Me Amadeus'?

27. The dance classic 'Ride on Time' was performed by which group?

28. Which album, featuring a shiny steel guitar on its blue cover, was the biggest selling album by a UK band in the eighties?

29. *Songs from the Big Chair* was a top-selling album for which band?

30. 'It's Christmas time and there's no need to be afraid,' was the opening line of which massive charity single?

31. Which singer made a transatlantic trip to play at both the British and the American Live Aid shows?

32. Was 'Atomic', 'Call Me' or 'The Tide is High' Blondie's first number one single of the 1980s?

33. With which band did Olivia Newton John record a relatively successful album, but an unsuccessful film called *Xanadu*?

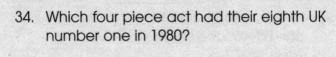

34. Which four piece act had their eighth UK number one in 1980?

35. Which much-loved US show's theme tune made number one in the UK during 1980?

36. Which band had chart success with 'Love Plus One', and were fronted by toothy singer, Nick Heyward?

37. Which school choir sang 'There's No One Quite Like Grandma'?

38. Which British act won Eurovision in 1981 with a routine involving skirts being whipped-off?

39. What was Adam and the Ants' first number one single?

40. Who co-wrote the original Band Aid single with Bob Geldof and produced the record?

41. Which group collaborated with David Bowie on the song 'Under Pressure'?

42. What was the name of the group of Caribbean singers, led by a fire-eating German, who had a hit with 'Seven Tears' in 1982?

43. Which smooth Spanish singer had a major hit with 'Begin the Beguine'?

44. What track was Wham's fourth and last UK number one?

45. Susanne Sulley and Joanne Catherall joined which group in 1981?

46. Which duo did Alison Moyet play in before going solo?

47. What was the name of the song that gave ABBA their last UK number one single in the eighties?

48. What was the name of the song recorded as an American response to Band Aid?

49. What did the celebrities who recorded it name themselves?

50. Which American band released the albums *Stop Making Sense*, *True Stories* and *Little Creatures* during the 1980s?

SPORT

1. Where were the 1988 Olympic Games held: South Korea, Spain or the United States?

2. Who shattered the 100 metres sprinting world record in 1988 only to be discovered using drugs?

3. Which British decathlete won gold at the 1980 and 1984 Olympics?

4. Which British pair won three world figure skating championships?

5. Which English football team won the 1981 UEFA Cup?

6. Which Canadian snooker player was famous for drinking a number of pints of beer before and during a match to steady his hands?

7. If you were watching Big Cliff Lazarenko vanquish Leighton Rees in the 1980s, what sport would you have been watching?

8. Which Olympic middle distance runner and gold medallist of the eighties became a Conservative MP in the nineties?

9. Did Graham Fowler, Chris Broad or David Gower score the largest Test Match innings by an English player during the 1980s?

10. Which football team won the 1981 English League Championship?

11. Which American boxer had the nickname 'The Hit Man'?

12. How many times did John McEnroe win the Wimbledon Men's Singles title?

13. Aberdeen, Celtic and Rangers won nine of the decade's Scottish league championships. Which side won the other one?

14. The first ever Rugby World Cup was held in New Zealand and Australia but in which year?

15. Juventus knocked which English football team out of the semi-finals of the European Cup Winners' Cup in 1983-1984?

16. Which England rugby union forward was a police constable and played club rugby for Preston Grasshoppers: Paul Ackford, Wade Dooley, Peter Winterbottom or Paul Rendall?

17. Which goalkeeper was part of the England football squad at both the 1982 and 1986 World Cup finals?

18. What number shirt did Gary Lineker tend to wear when playing for England?

19. Which Alex Ferguson-managed team won the 1983 European Cup Winners' Cup?

20. In what year did rower Steve Redgrave win his first Olympic gold medal?

21. Who won his fourth US Open at the age of 40, in 1980?

22. Where were the 1980 Summer Olympics held?

23. Which England fast bowler demolished Australia in the second innings of the 1981 Headingley Test?

24. Who was the only Grand Prix driver to win back-to-back World Championships during the 1980s?

25. What nationality was the driver?

26. Were the 1980 Winter Olympics held in Innsbruck, Lake Placid or Grenoble?

27. Which javelin thrower was BBC Sports Personality of the Year in 1987: Steve Backley, Tessa Sanderson or Fatima Whitbread?

28. Which Australian batsman scored more test cricket runs than any other player during the 1980s?

29. The 1988 FA Cup final saw a shock win for which team over favourites Liverpool?

30. Which Welsh rugby union fly-half moved into rugby league, playing for Widnes in 1989?

31. Which Welsh snooker player was world number one in 1982-1983 and was nicknamed 'Dracula'?

32. Did Everton, Liverpool or Arsenal win the 1989 English League Championship?

33. Which darts player won his first World Championship in 1980 and was nicknamed the 'Crafty Cockney'?

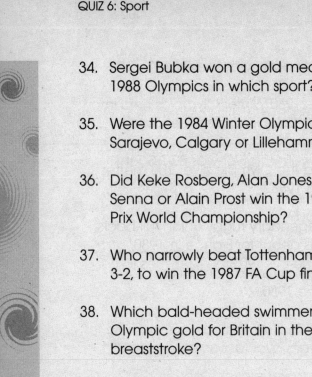

34. Sergei Bubka won a gold medal at the 1988 Olympics in which sport?

35. Were the 1984 Winter Olympics held in Sarajevo, Calgary or Lillehammer?

36. Did Keke Rosberg, Alan Jones, Ayrton Senna or Alain Prost win the 1982 Grand Prix World Championship?

37. Who narrowly beat Tottenham Hotspur 3-2, to win the 1987 FA Cup final?

38. Which bald-headed swimmer won a 1980 Olympic gold for Britain in the 100 metres breaststroke?

39. In which European country was the 1982 football World Cup held?

40. Mike Brearley regained the England cricket captaincy from which player in 1981?

41. Where were the 1984 Summer Olympics held?

42. Which Indian tennis player of the 1980s went on to act in James Bond movies?

43. Kevin Keegan left Liverpool to play football in which country?

44. Jackie Joyner-Kersee was an eighties legend in which sport: heptathlon, ice-skating, gymnastics or tennis?

45. Which British sprinter was eventually awarded the Olympic silver 100 metres medal in 1988?

46. Which legendary rugby union full-back made his debut for France in 1980, and made over 90 appearances for his country?

47. Which British figure skater won Olympic gold in 1980?

48. Which snooker player reached eight world championship finals during the 1980s?

49. Who won the Ashes cricket series in 1981 three matches to one?

50. In which year did the United States team lose the Ryder Cup for the first time since 1957?

FILMS AND FILM STARS

1. If you were watching the Ice Man play beach volleyball in between flying jet fighters, what film would you have been watching?

2. What was the first Indiana Jones film?

3. Which Oscar-winning film starred Tom Cruise and Dustin Hoffman as brothers?

4. Mel Gibson and Danny Glover co-starred in which 1987 action film?

5. What was the name of the 1984 comedy film, which achieved a massive cult following, about a fictional failing British heavy metal band?

6. If you saw Marty McFly time travelling into the past and trying to avoid the attentions of his mother, what film were you watching?

7. Which film was released first: *Beverley Hills Cop, Airplane* or *Spies Like Us*?

8. Who starred as the cocktail waiter in the eighties film *Cocktail*?

9. 1980 saw the release of *Superman II*. Who played Superman's enemy, Lex Luthor?

10. What was the second film in the *Star Wars* series to reach cinema audiences?

11. What was the name of the sequel to *Alien* released in 1986?

12. 'Love Lifts Us Up Where We Belong' was the rousing theme tune to which early 1980s romantic film?

13. Who starred alongside Tom Cruise in *Days of Thunder*?

14. Who starred as a shipwrecked girl in the 1980 film *Blue Lagoon*?

15. Who married screen actress Melanie Griffith, for the second time in 1989?

16. Which film, featuring a cute, big-eyed alien, was advertised with the line, 'The Story that Touched the World'?

17. Which future *Batman* actor played a house-husband in the comedy *Mr Mum*?

18. What was the full name of Sly Stallone's character in the 1985 film *First Blood Part II*?

19. Which 1987 film mirrored the greed of stockmarkets and finance of the time and featured Michael Douglas and Charlie Sheen?

20. Which 1989 Spike Lee film featured Lee as the pizza delivery man called Mookie?

21. Which 1988 comic horror film directed by Tim Burton, featured a young Wynona Ryder in the cast?

22. Which film featured Robert De Niro as middleweight boxer Jake LaMotta?

23. Can you name the 1981 film which starred Henry Fonda and Katherine Hepburn, both in their seventies?

24. Which 1989 drama featured Robin Williams as a lecturer called Mr Keating?

25. Which member of the eighties TV show *Cheers*, starred in *Three Men and a Baby*?

26. Which 1987 romantic film grossed over 100 million pounds and launched the career of Patrick Swayze?

27. Michael Caine won a Best Supporting Actor Oscar for which 1986 film?

28. What 1980 British film featured John Gordon Sinclair as a gawky football goalkeeper in love with the team's female recruit?

29. Which actor was found in all the following eighties movies: *48 Hours, Coming to America, The Golden Child* and *Harlem Nights*?

30. Which American actress won her first Oscar in 1988 for her role in the film *The Accused*?

31. Two popular 1987 films, *Raising Arizona* and *Moonstruck,* featured the acting talents of which male lead?

32. Which award-winning period drama starred John Malkovich and Glenn Close, and was set in Paris in the late eighteenth century?

33. Which Oliver Stone movie about war won the 1986 Best Film Oscar?

34. In the first Indiana Jones film, which legendary Biblical artefact was Indiana Jones seeking?

35. Which 1983 film featured Eddie Murphy as Billie Ray Valentine, a homeless con-man who is suddenly propelled into rich society?

36. Which popular film featured the character Harry Burns, a born pessimist played by Billy Crystal?

37. Can you name the actor who played the comic lead in both *Big* and *Splash* during the eighties?

38. Which actress and comic's first major screen role was in *The Colour Purple*?

39. Which actor won an Oscar nomination for his portrayal of a white police officer in the 1988 film *Mississippi Burning*, a film about racial prejudice in the USA's Deep South?

40. 'Greed is good' was a memorable line from which of the following films: *The Big Chill, Days of Thunder, Wall Street* or *Brewster's Millions*?

41. 'I am serious. And don't call me Shirley' was an immortal line from which 1980 comedy film?

42. If you were watching an unconventional black police officer stick bananas up an exhaust pipe, what film would you be viewing?

43. Which film featured a relentless killing machine from the future trying to murder the character Sarah Conner?

44. Which film featured Ferris, his girlfriend Sloane and his best friend Cameroon, as they skip school?

45. Who played Vicki Vale in the 1989 *Batman* movie?

46. Which 1988 film featured a couple, played by Alec Baldwin and Geena Davis, who become ghosts and seek demonic help to keep their old house the same?

47. Can you name the film that featured the Jock, the Brain, the Criminal, the Princess, and the Kook who all sat out a lengthy detention in which they bared their souls to each other?

48. Who played the female singer that bewitched the Fabulous Baker Boys?

49. Who out of the following was not in the cast of *Hannah and her Sisters*: Carrie Fisher, Michael Caine, Mia Farrow, Diane Keaton or Barbara Hershey?

50. If you were watching Nigel Tufnell explain about his guitar collection and his amp which goes up to 11, what film would you be watching?

ARTS AND ENTERTAINMENT

1. Who wrote *The Satanic Verses*?

2. Whose painting, *The Irises*, sold for a sum reputed to be over 50 million US dollars in 1987?

3. Which musical featured a cast on rollerskates?

4. Which British novelist won the 1983 Nobel Prize for Literature: William Golding, Kingsley Amis or Iris Murdoch?

5. Who wrote the book *Spycatcher*?

6. If you were reading a book containing the characters Slartibartfast and Zaphod Beeblebrox, who was the author?

7. Which historical figure's diaries proved to be a fake during the 1980s, but not before *The Sunday Times* was duped into printing extracts?

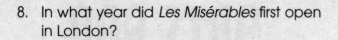

8. In what year did *Les Misérables* first open in London?

9. Amy Tan's *The Joy Luck Club*, was a bestselling novel about women's lives in which country?

10. An Egyptian, Polish, Spanish or Icelandic novelist won the 1988 Nobel Prize for Literature?

11. What London arts centre opened in 1983?

12. Whose book, *A History of the World in $10\frac{1}{2}$ Chapters*, became required reading at the end of the 1980s?

13. In which American city did graffiti art in subways rise to prominence in the early eighties?

14. Which Spanish surrealist artist died in 1989?

15. In 1987, what replaced the offensive black gollywogs in Enid Blyton stories?

16. Which moral guardian brought a court case against the play *Romans* for its male sex scenes, in the early 1980s?

17. Which of the following books was not written by Catherine Cookson, the bestselling women's author of the 1980s: *Tilley Trotter, A Dinner of Herbs, A Question of Honour* or *Bill Bailey*?

18. Which early eighties play about a contemporary of Mozart's later became a film starring F. Murray Abraham?

19. Which musical about a murderous barber opened in 1980 with Sheila Hancock in the original cast?

20. What famous Manchester nightclub opened for the first time in 1983?

21. Which novelist had the books *Cujo, It* and *Firestarter* all in the 1980s bestseller lists?

22. Which author won the Pulitzer Prize for his novel *Rabbit is Rich*?

23. Which Andrew Lloyd-Webber musical first opened in London in 1989?

24. Salman Rushdie won the Booker Prize for which book in 1981?

25. Which author wrote *First Light, Chatterton* and *Hawksmoor* during the 1980s?

26. What was the second book in *The Hitchhiker's Guide to the Galaxy* called?

27. In front of which famous Paris museum did architect I.M. Pei construct a large glass pyramid?

28. What music venue, synonymous with the Beatles, was bulldozed in the mid-1980s?

29. Whose book, *The Commitments*, was later made into a popular movie?

30. What was the name of the venue around which alternative stand-up comedy grew in the early 1980s?

31. Kazuo Ishiguro won the 1989 Booker Prize with *The Remains of the Day, An Artist of the Floating World* or *The Unconsoled*?

32. Who described the design of an extension to the National Gallery in London as a 'monstrous carbuncle'?

33. Did Kingsley Amis, Martin Amis or Margaret Attwood win the 1986 Booker Prize with their novel, *The Old Devils*?

34. Judy Blume's 1981 book was called *Supergran, Superfudge* or *Superdog*?

35. What was the original title of Thomas Keneally's 1982 Booker Prize-winning novel, later made into an Oscar-winning film by Steven Spielberg?

36. Richard Rogers was the architect of which City of London building that opened its doors in 1986?

37. Which female author wrote *Nuns and Soldiers* and *The Good Apprentice* during the 1980s?

38. Which musical adaptation of a Gaston Leroux novel opened in London, in 1987?

39. Who became Poet Laureate in 1984: Seamus Heaney, Ted Hughes or Peter Porter?

40. What was the name of the play by David Mamet that won a Pulitzer Prize in 1984?

41. Whose book, *Executioner's Song*, examined the life of murderer Gary Gilmore?

42. Which Andrew Lloyd Webber musical opened in 1980?

43. *The Colour Purple* was written by Angela Morrison, Alice Walker or Alanis Milton?

44. Which playwright completed his celebrated work, *The Singing Detective*, in 1985?

45. Who wrote *The Hunt for Red October* and *Red Storm Rising* during the 1980s?

46. Who was the author of the 1984 novel *The Witches of Eastwick*?

47. What was the name of the American astronomer whose book, Cosmos, topped non-fiction bestseller lists during the early 1980s?

48. *Les Misérables* opened for the first time in Paris in 1980, 1985 or 1989?

49. Which celebrated political cartoonist started producing his If cartoon strip in the *Guardian* newspaper from 1981?

50. Which comedy film maker and star was a member of the original line-up of The Comedy Store players who first entertained audiences in London in 1985?

EVENTS

1. What fell on the 9th November 1989?

2. Which religious figure was shot in May 1981?

3. Which American motor company went bankrupt in 1982: Delorean, General Motors or Cadillac?

4. Which President of Yugoslavia died in 1980?

5. Which country's forces invaded the Falkland Islands in 1982?

6. Which country invaded Afghanistan at the start of the 1980s?

7. Over which country did a Pan-Am airliner explode in 1988?

8. Which London Underground station was the scene of a devastating fire in 1987?

9. What was the former name of the African nation of Zimbabwe that achieved independence in 1980?

10. In 1980, which US volcano underwent a major eruption?

11. In which US state was this volcano found?

12. Did John McCarthy remain kidnapped for one year, two years, four years or over five years?

13. In what year did Black Monday cause massive losses on the stock markets?

14. How many miles long was the 1983 chain, formed by CND supporters to protest against the siting of Cruise Missiles at Greenham Common: three, four, 14 or 24 miles?

15. A pornography star was elected into which country's parliament in 1987?

16. Can you name the district of Liverpool in which race riots erupted in 1981?

17. What was the name of the space shuttle that propelled the first American woman into space in 1983?

18. In 1986, a fire started by a bedside candle devastated parts of which historic building near London?

19. In which year did the world population exceed five billion for the first time?

20. In which Middle Eastern city were 216 people killed by a suicide bomb in 1983?

21. What was the name of the Argentinian cruiser sunk by British forces in 1982, causing the loss of 321 lives?

22. Which war in the Middle East lasted between 1980 and 1988, with at least a million lives lost as a result?

23. US troops invaded which Caribbean island in 1983?

24. Who became the first female leader of the Philippines in 1986?

25. The Soviet Union shot down an aircraft from which airline in 1983, killing 269 passengers?

26. Which country's capital city of Beirut became a place of war during the 1980s?

27. In which Peking square did major student and civil protests occur in 1989?

28. What Russian policy of openness was instituted by Mikhail Gorbachev in the mid- to late 1980s?

29. Who became leader of Zimbabwe in 1980?

30. 52 US hostages were released after 444 days in captivity from which country?

31. In what year were the hostages released?

32. Anwar el-Sadat was assassinated in 1981: which country was he leader of at the time?

33. In what year did Spain's first democratic elections since the 1930s occur?

34. Militant Tendency were a group found within which British political party in the 1980s?

35. In which American city did the Reverend Sun Myung Moon marry 2,075 couples in a 1982 mass wedding?

36. Terrorists from which country were suspected of planting the bomb that destroyed an American airliner over Lockerbie in 1988?

37. What was the name of the Indian Prime Minister who was murdered in 1984?

38. Was Yuri Andropov, Boris Yeltsin or Konstantin Chernenko leader of the Soviet Union until his death in 1985?

39. Mikhail Gorbachev met which world leader for the first time in Geneva in 1985?

40. Which country changed its name to Myanmar in 1989?

41. Who became leader of the Labour Party in 1983?

42. Did 15, 25, 35 or 45 nations boycott the 1980 Olympics, in protest at the Soviet Union's invasion of Afghanistan?

43. Olaf Palme, was Prime Minister of which European country when he was murdered in February 1986?

44. Which year saw the deaths of Emperor Hirohito, Sir Laurence Olivier, Bette Davis and Mel Blanc, the voice of Bugs Bunny?

45. In which year did the space shuttle, Challenger, explode in mid-air?

46. Which country withdrew from Cambodia in 1989 after a decade of occupation?

47. Who became President of the United States following the 1988 election?

48. Who did he defeat in the 1988 election?

49. Where did West German teenager Matthias Rust manage to land his light aircraft in 1987?

50. Which major American landmark underwent a massive renovation programme in the mid-1980s?

TELEVISION

1. Which American show featured a private detective basking in a lodge on the grounds of millionaire author, Robin Masters' estate in Hawaii?

2. Which British soap motel burned down in 1981?

3. Which eighties cop show gave a leading role to the actor who had been *Star Trek's* Captain Kirk?

4. Which cards-based quiz featured Bruce Forsythe and an audience screaming 'higher' or 'lower'?

5. What was the name of the onboard computer on the *Red Dwarf* spaceship?

6. Which cop show paired a tough, impetuous New York cop with Lady Harriet, a young English aristocrat with a Cambridge science degree?

7. Which gritty drama featured the life of Yosser Hughes and his peers?

8. Which one of the following was not a *The Comic Strip Presents* feature: A Fistful of Travellers Cheques, Bad News Tour, Dead at Thirty or Strike!?

9. In which American city was CHiPs set?

10. David Healey and Mark Healey become the partners of the two Conner sisters in which American sitcom?

11. In which year did Grace Brothers finally close, and *Are You Being Served?* leave our screens?

12. Can you name two of the four children Blake and Alexis had in *Dynasty*?

13. If you were watching Tinker check out some antiques, which popular show would you be viewing?

14. Which drama about the Sun Hill police force was first broadcast in 1984?

15. Which innovative cop show featured a public defender called Joyce Davenport and Sergeant Phil Esterhaus who read out a roll call at the start of each show?

16. What was the name of the character in *Moonlighting* played by Cybill Shepherd?

17. Who was Rodney Trotter's best mate: Uncle Albert, Mickey Pearce or Mike the barman?

18. What was the name of the American show which featured the goings-on at St Eligius teaching hospital?

19. *A Kick Up the 80s* featured Rik Mayall performing his Alan B'stard character, his Kevin Turvey character or his Rick from *The Young Ones* character?

20. Which Harry Enfield character emerged near the end of the eighties waving large amounts of banknotes around?

21. Which *Blankety Blank* guest frequently bent Terry Wogan's stick microphone: Isla St Clair, Kenny Everett, Frank Carson or Beryl Reid?

22. What American show would you have been watching if you viewed the antics of Elaine, Alex, Latka, Tony and the 'Reverend' Jim?

23. Which quiz show hosted by Jim Bowen saw contestants throw darts and answer questions in order to compete for Bully's Star Prize?

24. Which slow-witted *Only Fools and Horses* character always called Rodney, 'Dave'?

25. If you asked Bob Holness for 'a C please', what 1980s quiz show were you a contestant in?

26. Can you give the first names of all four of *The Young Ones*?

27. What was the name of the ranch in *Dallas*?

28. At the end of the seventh series of *Minder*, Terry, played by Dennis Waterman, moved to which foreign country?

29. What was the name of the raunchy character played by Rik Mayall who appeared in series two and series four of *Blackadder*?

30. What eighties show was a spin-off from *Dallas* and featured Gary and Valene Ewing?

31. Which sitcom, featuring Keith Barron, was about two English couples on a seemingly permanent holiday in Spain: *They Don't Make the Tea, Costa Capers, Sunburn* or *Duty Free*?

32. Whose Madhouse TV show featured characters including Basildon Bond, C.U. Jimmy and Cooperman?

33. Beth Davenport and police lieutenant Dennis Becker, were two of which private detective's close friends?

34. Which British soap started in the early 1980s when much of the drama was centred round the lives of the Grant family?

35. Can you name both police motorcyclists from the show CHiPs?

36. Can you name any one of the four contestants from Footlights College, Oxbridge in *The Young Ones'* anarchic version of *University Challenge*?

37. Who was the youngest of the Walton children: Jim-Bob, Mary Ellen or Elizabeth?

38. Lady Jane Felsham was the love interest for which rogue antiques dealer in the 1980s?

39. If you were watching an alien living among humans, greeting you with the phrase 'Nanu Nanu', what show were you watching?

40. What was the name of the comedy show featuring two members of the *Not the Nine O'Clock News* quartet, which often featured the pair silhouetted head to head?

41. Which soap opera started with Daphne springing out of a cake during Des's buck's party?

42. Which detective show, set on the island of Jersey, featured the work and life of Charlie Hungerford's former son-in-law?

43. What was the name of the character in *Moonlighting* played by Bruce Willis?

44. David Jacob Conner's father is called Dan and his aunt is called Jackie. What show is he from and what is he usually called?

45. *The Bill's* very first episode focused on a young copper's first day on the beat. The character was still in *The Bill* nearly twenty years later, can you name him?

46. How many letters do contestants pick in the quiz show *Countdown*, which first aired in 1982?

47. Can you name one of the two characters who were usually found in the court of Queen Elizabeth when *Blackadder* visited?

48. What was the name of the butler, played by David Jason, in the hit drama *Porterhouse Blue*?

49. What was the name of the man mountain in *Auf Wiedersehen, Pet*, played by former wrestler, Pat Roach?

50. What was the name of the sitcom featuring the character John Lacey trying to rebuild his life after his wife had left him?

LIFE

1. If you and your friends were young upwardly mobile professionals in the mid-1980s, what were you nicknamed?

2. What sort of low-lying wooden bed became popular in the eighties: the divan, the futon or the sofabed?

3. In which city was the Fares Fair policy introduced only to be banned in the courts?

4. What colour was the British pound note which was phased out of circulation during the 1980s?

5. What was replaced by GCSEs in 1986?

6. Work began on which transport link between Britain and Europe in 1986?

7. Which Scandinavian company opened its first UK store in 1987?

8. Which airline collapsed in 1982 with debts of over 250 million pounds?

9. Who was leader of the National Union of Mineworkers during the Miner's Strike of the mid-1980s?

10. In what year was caning and other corporal punishment banned from British schools?

11. The Sinclair C5 electric battery-driven car went on sale in the 1980s for: £399, £899, £1299 or £1599?

12. Which new music format became available from 1983 onwards?

13. What was the commonly used nickname for the Community Charge, introduced by the Conservative Government at the end of the 1980s?

14. What diary-like object became a must-have for Yuppies in the mid-1980s?

15. In what year did the BBC's *Breakfast Television* programme start broadcasting?

16. In 1987, a driverless, computer-controlled public railway was opened, but where in Britain was it situated?

17. What famous location in Cornwall was sold for seven million pounds in 1987?

18. In what year did Channel 4 first appear on British television screens?

19. What was the first programme Channel 4 showed?

20. In what year was it announced that the Greater London Council was to be abolished?

21. Which American TV news station began broadcasting in 1980?

22. Which 1980s chocolate biscuit bar advertised itself as five treats in one bar?

23. What coin ceased to be legal tender in the early 1980s?

24. Which of the following acts was the first to release an album on compact disc: Billy Joel, Pink Floyd or Culture Club?

25. The pound coin was introduced into Britain in which year?

26. What was sold in litres for the first time in Britain in 1981?

27. Which diet, written by Audrey Eaton, was released in 1982 and suggested high fibre foods and only 1,000 calories a day?

28. In which year did cordless telephones for the home first arrive in Britain?

29. In what year was Britain battered by the worst storms in more than 250 years?

30. In 1983, wheel-clamping of illegally-parked cars began in which British city?

31. Can you recall the name of the IRA prisoner who went on hunger strike, was elected as an MP and died in 1981?

32. At what church were Prince Charles and Lady Diana married?

33. What snack, launched by Golden Wonder at the very start of the 1980s, needed just hot water to transform itself into a hot meal?

34. Who was the last leader of the Greater London Council?

35. What was the name of the first colour-printed newspaper which was launched in Britain in 1986?

36. Which part of London was massively regenerated during the 1980s, including the building of Canary Wharf and Hays Galleria?

37. In which country was the Poll Tax first introduced: England, Scotland, Wales or Northern Ireland?

38. If you were trying to 'moonwalk' backwards in the playground, which singer were you trying to impersonate?

39. In what year was the National Curriculum introduced for schools?

40. The first new broadsheet of the 1980s was launched in 1986. What was it called?

41. 'How do you eat yours?' was an advertising campaign started in 1985 for which sweet product?

42. Which one of the following was not a *Choose Your Own Adventure* gamebook author in the 1980s: Stephen Thraves, Ian Livingstone or Mark Allen?

43. What was the name given to a type of street dancing which saw the most talented dancers able to spin around on their heads?

44. What name was given to upper class young Londoners taken from a handbook by Peter York?

45. 1981 saw the introduction of the Quenchers range of ice-lollies. One of the flavours was cherry: can you recall either of the others?

46. What enhancement to toothpaste packaging was first introduced in 1984?

47. What colour Smarties were first introduced in 1989?

48. What sort of furniture, used to eat your food off in the morning, appeared in many eighties kitchens?

49. Trendy teen girl speech and slang from California became popular for a short while in the UK during the eighties. What was this form of speech called?

50. Which year of the eighties was the warmest on record up to that point?

MUSIC

1. Which band's celebration of soul and blues singer Geno Washington, launched their career?

2. Which band sang about 'Echo Beach' at the start of the decade?

3. Which song by Jackie Wilson was first recorded in 1957 but was a major hit in 1986?

4. Jan Hammer had a major instrumental hit in 1985 with the theme tune from which popular American cop show?

5. From which city did the young band Musical Youth emerge?

6. Julian Cope led which band, known for its single 'Reward' and the albums *Kilimanjaro* and *Wilder*?

7. Which rappers became famous for their songs 'White Lines' and 'The Jungle'?

8. What was the name of the singer from Kajagoogoo with flamboyant hair?

9. Which Scottish female singer had hits with 'Modern Girl' and '9 to 5', and also sang the theme tune to the Bond movie *For Your Eyes Only*?

10. Which singer had her first major hit with 'All Around the World' in 1989?

11. How many number one singles did Jive Bunny manage during the 1980s?

12. Which influential band's first single was 'Hand in Glove'?

13. Which American singer had a massive chart hit with 'Girls Just Wanna Have Fun': Debbie Gibson, Cyndi Lauper or Teena Marie?

14. Which Swedish rock band had chart success with 'The Final Countdown' which featured an often-mimicked keyboard riff?

15. What theme tune, from the movie *Top Gun*, was sung by the band Berlin?

16. Which member of the Young Ones had single success with 'Hole in my Shoe'?

17. Which haunting track by Ultravox reached number two in the charts in 1981?

18. Which duo released the singles 'Bad Boys', 'Young Guns (Go for it)' and 'Club Tropicana'?

19. Can you recall Midge Ure's only number one single?

20. Which former member of Generation X had hits with 'Rebel Yell' and 'White Wedding'?

21. Which popular student band had a hit indie album, *Back in the DHSS*, which featured the tracks 'I Hate Nerys Hughes', 'The Len Ganley Stance' and '99 percent of Gargoyles Look Like Bob Todd'?

22. Who asked people to 'walk like an Egyptian' during the late 1980s?

23. Which massive New Romantic band's last UK live performance of the eighties was at the Live Aid concert?

24. What was the name of Paul Weller's group formed after the Jam split?

25. Who, in 1985, became the first female artist to hold the number one and number two chart single positions in the UK?

26. Which band recorded 'Jealous Guy' as a tribute to John Lennon?

27. Marti Pellow was lead singer of which Scottish soul band?

28. The British Electric Foundation (BEF) and Heaven 17 were both formed by members of which band?

29. Singer Ian Curtis hung himself in 1980. What name did his bandmates re-form under?

30. The lead singer of which Irish new wave band joined ex-Yazoo member Vince Clark, to help form the Assembly?

31. Was the group Ah-Ha: Norwegian, Swedish, Danish or Dutch?

32. Which Mancunian band featured the Ryder brothers on guitar and vocals?

33. What was the name of the final Smiths album released in 1987 after the band had already broken up?

34. With which rap band did Aerosmith collaborate for the monster hit 'Walk this Way'?

35. What was the name of the soft rockers who had a major hit with 'All Out of Love' in 1980?

36. Whose 1989 debut album was called *Raw Like Sushi*?

37. Which influential singer-songwriter released albums in the eighties including *Spike, King of America* and *Almost Blue*?

38. What was the name of the band that released 'Soul Mining' in 1983 and were joined by the Smiths' lead guitarist, Johnny Marr, in 1988?

39. Which American rock band's big breakthrough album was *Slippery When Wet*: Guns 'n' Roses, REO Speedwagon or Bon Jovi?

40. Whose debut single was 'Never Gonna Give You Up'?

41. Can you name the three record producers who provided hits for a legion of artists including Kylie Minogue, Jason Donovan and Mel and Kim?

42. Which power trio's drummer, Frank Beard, was the only member of the group without a long beard?

43. Which Heavy Metal band's 1982 album was called *Run to the Hills*: Ratt, Judas Priest, Iron Maiden or Spyder?

44. Who fronted Van Halen at the time of their huge smash 'Jump'?

45. Which member of Simple Minds married Chrissie Hynde of the Pretenders in 1987?

46. Who became the first artist to reach the US Top 20 with an aerobics record in 1983?

47. Was Curiosity Killed the Cat, Ah-Ha, King or Bronski Beat's debut album called *Keep Your Distance*?

48. Which white rap band was blamed for the theft of thousands of Volkswagen symbols from cars?

49. What year was the music show *The Tube's* last?

50. Can you name either of the two Pink Floyd albums containing new material released in the 1980s?

ADVERTISING

1. Which Australian actor advertised Fosters Lager in the 1980s?

2. Which soft drink was 'too orangey for crows'?

3. Which bank advertised itself as 'the bank that likes to say yes'?

4. What chocolate bar had 'a hazelnut in every bite'?

5. Which company first launched phonecards in Britain?

6. What soft drink in a carton was advertised with the slogan, 'they drink it in the Congo'?

7. What was the name of the elderly gentlemen searching for a book in the famous Yellow Pages advert?

8. Whose services and products were advertised by a series of plasticine animals under the name Creature Comforts?

9. Which tea bag brand 'let the flavour flood out'?

10. 'No, Luton Airport' was an advertising catchphrase spoken by which actress?

11. What product was she advertising?

12. Which company's adverts featured a woman talking about 'an ology'?

13. Which airline created an advert of a giant face made up of hundreds of people as viewed from the air?

14. Which member of the current cast of *Buffy the Vampire Slayer* first found fame as the romantic male lead in the Gold Blend adverts during the eighties?

15. Which TV personality fronted a series of adverts for Barclaycard during the eighties?

16. What song provided the soundtrack for the memorable Levi's launderette advert that featured a man stripping down to his boxer shorts?

17. 'Ullo Tosh' was a phrase used in which company's TV adverts?

18. Which beer did Griff Rhys Jones advertise in a series of black and white TV adverts?

19. Which ice cream product was advertised with a faux Italian opera song?

20. Which company's adverts featured people looking for Sid?

21. What was the name of the purple coloured cartoon characters which advertised a popular blackcurrant drink in the late 1980s?

22. What brand called its products the Rooster Booster from 1980 onwards?

23. Which comedian advertised Smith's Square Shaped Crisps?

24. Were there 100, 200, 500 or 2,000 perforations in every Tetley's tea bag according to the Tetley tea folk?

25. Which actress fronted a long series of adverts for BT in the 1980s?

26. Which newspaper was launched with the slogan 'It is. Are you'?

27. Which brand of beer's famous advert featured the Dambusters?

28. Which sportswear company had the early 1980s slogan, 'McEnroe swears by them'?

29. Which rap group wrote a song about their Adidas trainers?

30. Aardman Animations are most famous for their Wallace and Gromit films, but in which late 1980s advertising campaign did they first find fame?

31. Which perfume spray's adverts showed men so entranced by the fragrance that they instantly bought the woman flowers?

32. At what sort of event did Paul Hogan, advertising Fosters, exclaim, 'Strewth, that bloke's got no strides on!'?

33. What was the title of the book J.R. Hartley was searching for in the Yellow Pages TV advert?

34. What was the name of the bear that advertised Hofmeister Beer during the 1980s?

35. Which beer brand was being advertised if you were watching some Australian men load a pick-up truck with cases of lager and a single bottle of sherry?

36. What item was advertised with a cartoon of a man with a flip-top head?

37. Which new town advertised itself as 'if only all places were like...'?

38. If you were watching workmen in the back of a van singing, 'hope it's chips, it's chips', were you watching an advert for Birds Eye, Findus, Iceland or Tesco?

39. Adverts which warned viewers to be aware of expensive imitations, were for Sekonda watches, Stella Artois lager or Cockburns Port?

40. What savoury snack was advertised as the biggest snack pennies can buy?

41. Whose hair caught fire during the shooting of a 1984 Pepsi advert?

42. Which credit card promoted itself as 'your flexible friend' during the 1980s?

43. What German phrase was introduced into Britain by Audi's car advertising, from 1984 onwards?

44. What small chocolate bar was advertised as 'just enough to give your kids a treat'?

45. George Cole's Arthur Daley character, appeared in adverts for which Building Society: Abbey National, Bradford and Bingley, the Leeds or the Halifax?

46. Orangutans featured in adverts for Goodrich, Michelin or Uniroyal tyres?

47. Which home computer advertised itself as 'a computer capable of running a nuclear power station'?

48. Which chocolate bar, with an outlaw's name, was advertised by Bill Oddie?

49. Which grapefruit-flavoured fizzy drink was advertised as 'so cool, people's glasses froze over'?

50. Did Fish 'n' Chips, Outer Spacers or Wigwams come in pickled onion flavour?

FASHION AND FADS

1. Which ethical toiletries shop was set up by Anita Roddick?

2. What is the name of the TV series, based at The New York Academy of Performing Arts, that launched a million leg-warmer wearers?

3. What mid-eighties fashion boot with rubber soles mimicked astronauts' footwear?

4. Which company made the Air Max trainers which were in heavy demand in the late 1980s?

5. Which clothes shop for women first opened in February 1982: Next, Burtons, Dorothy Perkins or New Look?

6. Which of the following was not an eighties hair styling technique: crimping, shaving or scrunching?

7. What was the name of the plastic or rubber bracelets often worn in great numbers on arms?

8. What sort of male casual trousers became popular from the mid-1980s onwards?

9. What sort of black-clad fashion look did bands such as the Cure and Sisters of Mercy help promote in the 1980s?

10. Which pop singer starred in a celebrated video which spawned thousands of short red leather jacket wearers?

11. What sort of male hairstyle, short and spiky on top but long at the back, was popularised by footballers and pop stars during the 1980s?

12. Pastel coloured t-shirts worn underneath jackets rolled up at the sleeves were referred to as the Miami Vice, the Dynasty or the Dallas look?

13. Window ornaments and cuddly toys featuring which cartoon cat became popular during the eighties?

14. Which guitarist popularised the wearing of towelling headbands in the early 1980s?

15. Roos were a type of trainer with sewn-in velcro pockets, a type of luminous sock or a glitter-covered hairband?

16. Which pop singer popularised the wearing of jellies, crucifixes and underwear as outerwear?

17. What brand of plastic collectible watch was launched in the 1980s?

18. What type of big sunglasses were popularised by the *Top Gun* movie?

19. Which dance studios, set up in a disused warehouse in Covent Garden by Debbie Moore, had a great influence on exercise and exercise clothing during the 1980s?

20. What name was given to the short waist-length jacket with three-quarter length sleeves that was styled on a bullfighter's clothing?

21. Which designer popularised slogan t-shirts and wore an anti-missile t-shirt to number 10 Downing Street?

22. Who launched her Pirates and Romantics range of fashions which were popularised by Adam and the Ants?

23. MC Hammer pants were tight-fitting, baggy and metallic, or three-quarter length jeans?

24. What style of hair, popular with many in the 1980s, required a special tool to form minature waves?

25. Whose wedding dress featured 10,000 pearls, pearl sequins and an eight metre long train?

26. What was the surname of the designers David and Elizabeth?

27. Hugo Boss, Hamnett or Westwood were one of the key makers of men's jackets worn with the sleeves rolled up?

28. Which French clothing company pioneered the three button polo shirt?

29. Name three eighties films, all beginning with the letter F, which featured dancing and leg-warmers.

30. Which American actress helped kick start the fashion for aerobics with her workout video in 1982?

31. Which band produced a slogan t-shirt with 'Relax' printed in large letters?

32. Who launched their United Colours clothing range featuring striped t-shirts in the mid-1980s?

33. What was the alternative name for calf length trousers, also known as clam-diggers?

34. Which multi-layered short skirt became popular from 1982 onwards: minis, ra-ra skirts or frou-frou skirts?

35. What sort of sporting shorts became popular daywear in the late 1980s?

36. Crystal and Alexis were TV characters famous for their Mohican hairstyles, power suits with padded shoulders or denim jeans with bandanas around the knee?

37. Which American detective show sparked an eighties craze for Hawaiian shirts?

38. Which male designer opened the world's largest single designer store in 1986: Jean Paul Gautier, Ralph Lauren or Calvin Klein?

39. Did Kickers shoes, popular in the early 1980s, come from Germany, Belgium, the United States or France?

40. Next added children's wear, men's wear and interior furnishings to its stores during the eighties: which came first?

41. Where would you wear deelyboppers: on your feet, around your waist or on your head?

42. Did Madonna, the Human League or Boy George popularise the wearing of fingerless lace gloves?

43. Stonewashed jeans made their first appearance in the 1980s: true or false?

44. What sixties symbol was adopted as the fashion symbol for the Acid House movement?

45. What make of wax jacket, used in the country, was adopted in towns in the late 1980s?

46. The baggie music and clothing scene started in which British city: Liverpool, London, Sheffield or Manchester?

47. If you wore white stripes across your face, which pop star were you mimicking?

48. What sort of thin tracksuit in garish colours became popular in the late 1980s?

49. What type of Latin dance, beginning with the letter C, became a popular pastime during the 1980s?

50. Popular in the eighties, the rat-tail was a type of tight stonewashed jeans, a narrow metal studded belt or a small braided piece of hair?

SPORT

1. Which athlete ran middle distance races for Britain in bare feet during the 1980s?

2. Who won the darts world title five times in the 1980s?

3. Did England or Australia win the 1985 Ashes series?

4. Who scored two 1986 World Cup goals against England, including the famous 'Hand of God' goal?

5. Who, in 1985, became the youngest winner of the Wimbledon Men's Singles title?

6. Which Irishman, wearing his trademark 'upside-down' glasses, beat Steve Davis in the 1985 World Championship final watched by over 18 million people?

7. Which dynamic midfielder was nicknamed 'Captain Marvel'?

8. Which British female tennis player reached the world top five in the 1980s?

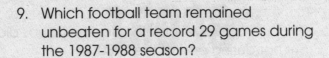

9. Which football team remained unbeaten for a record 29 games during the 1987-1988 season?

10. Which English darts player managed a perfect nine-dart 501 finish on television in 1984?

11. Which English football team won the 1982 European Cup: Liverpool, Aston Villa or Newcastle United?

12. Did Niki Lauda, Alain Prost or Nigel Mansell win the 1984 Grand Prix World Championship?

13. Which boxer, nicknamed 'Marvellous', demolished Britain's Alan Minter in a World Championship fight?

14. Who won the Wimbledon Ladies' Singles title for six years in a row during the 1980s?

15. Against which team did Gary Lineker score a hat-trick in the 1986 World Cup?

16. In which sport did Sean Kerly win a team Olympic gold medal at the 1988 games?

17. At what stage of the 1986 World Cup did England get knocked out by Argentina?

18. What novel feature did QPR, Oldham and Luton have which other football clubs did not during part of the 1980s?

19. What was the nationality of the leading wicket taker in Test Match cricket during the 1980s: West Indian, New Zealand, Australian or English?

20. Ayrton Senna won three Grand Prix World Championships during the 1980s. Can you name the other Brazilian who also won the World Championship during this decade?

21. Which American Olympic diver hit his head on the board during the 1988 games yet went on to win gold?

22. Which South American team did England beat 3-0 in the 1986 World Cup?

23. Who knocked England out of the first Rugby World Cup?

24. Which American athlete mirrored Jesse Owens' achievements by winning four gold medals in track and field events at the 1984 Olympics?

25. Which Scottish footballer did Liverpool buy to replace Kevin Keegan?

26. Joan Benoit won the women's Olympic javelin, the marathon or the 400 metre hurdles competition in 1984?

27. Boxing promoter Barry Hearn signed-up many of the 1980s leading snooker players including Steve Davis. What was the name of his group of stars?

28. At which Olympics did Steve Ovett and Sebastian Coe battle against each other in the 800 metres and 1,500 metres, each winning a gold medal?

29. Who scored in the very first minute of England's opening 1982 World Cup match against France?

30. Which British racing driver made his Grand Prix debut in a Lotus-Ford in 1980?

31. Which famous piece of music did Torvill and Dean dance to when they won the 1984 figure skating gold at the Olympics?

32. What was the name of John McEnroe's doubles partner?

33. Which England batsman scored three centuries when England retained the Ashes in 1986-1987: Mike Gatting, Chris Broad or David Gower?

34. Did Mark Spitz, Matt Biondi, Tom Jager or Alex Goss win five swimming gold medals at the 1988 Olympics?

35. The 1988 Olympics saw tennis, golf, cricket or football return to the games for the first time in many years?

36. Can you name either of the teams England had 0-0 draws with in the 1982 World Cup which meant that they could not qualify for the semi-finals?

37. Which football team won the English League Championship six times during the 1980s?

38. Which Pakistani batsman scored the two highest individual scores in test cricket during the 1980s?

39. Which popular Australian climbed up the Centre Court arena to celebrate winning Wimbledon in 1987?

40. Who was England manager for the 1982 World Cup: Don Revie, Bobby Robson or Ron Greenwood?

41. Which French Grand Prix driver achieved the vast majority of his 33 poll positions during the 1980s?

42. Which popular striker wore the number seven shirt for England in the 1982 World Cup?

43. Which Canadian snooker player gained the first maximum break in the World Championships in 1983?

44. Did Motherwell, St Mirren, Celtic or Rangers win the 1987 Scottish Cup?

45. Which Scottish sprinter won the 100 metres at the 1980 Olympics Games?

46. Can you name the legendary Italian goalkeeper who was 40 years of age when he lifted the 1982 World Cup?

47. Which team did England beat in the final to win the 1988 Olympic hockey gold?

48. Which Canadian snooker player famously split his trousers on live television while leaning over the table to play a shot?

49. Did Everton, Liverpool or Arsenal win the 1985 English League Championship?

50. Which male tennis player announced his shock retirement from the sport in 1983?

KIDS' TELEVISION

1. Which ten-minute long animated show focused on a road which featured Dr Glossop, Mr Jupiter the astronomer, William the window cleaner and Long Distance Clara, among others?

2. Over which eye did Dangermouse wear a patch?

3. Arnold and Kimberley were children in which popular American comedy?

4. Which much-loved entertainer hosted *Cartoon Time* on the BBC in the early 1980s?

5. What was the name of the show about a hapless detective whose cases were solved by his niece, Penny, with her talking computer book and her dog called Brain?

6. What was the full name of the Fonz?

7. Which show featured a comic witch who got all her magic powers from special tea grown by a magical plant?

8. Which ex-*Swap Shop* and *Saturday Superstore* presenter hosted his own pop quiz for children in the 1980s?

9. Which TV show featured Bryan Brown as a backwards-talking alien, a currency called Drogna and also featured Moira Stewart and Lesley Judd as co-hosts?

10. Which show pitted school sports teams against each other in running, swimming and obstacle games and was hosted by athletics commentator, Ron Pickering?

11. Who was the original main presenter of *Going Live*, the successor to *Saturday Superstore*?

12. Trevor Cleaver, Gripper Stebson, Pogo Patterson and Roland Browning: which two of these *Grange Hill* characters had ginger hair?

13. Which of the following were characters in the cartoon show *Henry's Cat*: Pansy Pig, Ted Tortoise, Harry Hare, Chris Rabbit or Sid Swallow?

14. In which continent was the Terrahawks' base, Hawknest, located?

15. What was the name of the spin-off series from *Grange Hill* charting the fortunes of some of the first series of pupils?

16. Did *Knightmare, Dungeons and Dragons* or *The Adventure Game* feature a dungeon master called Treguard?

17. What was the name of the puppy who joined *Scooby-Do* for adventures throughout the 1980s?

18. What show were you watching if you viewed the antics of Howling Mad Murdock and Face?

19. Which children's quiz show, hosted by Richard Stilgoe, featured children playing a form of battleship games for prizes?

20. Which cartoon superhero lived in a red pillar box outside the Baker Street home of Sherlock Holmes?

21. Which cartoon show about robots which could transform themselves into vehicles, was supported by toys and other merchandise made by Tonka?

22. Posy, Perkin and Pootle were all members of which show?

23. The actor who gave us Mama Smurf's voice in the 1980s cartoon was also the voice of Scooby-Do: true or false?

24. Who defended Etheria from Horak, armed with the Sword of Protection and the help of friends including Swift Wind and Madame Razz?

25. Which cartoon vampire bird preferred broccoli sandwiches to blood?

26. Which Gerry Anderson show from the 1960s was constantly repeated in the 1980s and featured Captain Steve Zodiac and Doctor Venus?

27. Which show featured the adventures of a lion, a mole called Rigadon and a mouse called Teeko travelling the planet?

28. Which one of the following was not an ally of He-Man: Stratos, Fisto, Mightius or Man-e-Faces?

29. Which cartoon doctor had among his friends: Dennis the Badger, a robot called Mathilda Junkbottom and Miss Nettles, his housekeeper?

30. Which *Star Wars* characters got their own cartoon in the mid-1980s?

31. Paula Yates and Jools Holland were key presenters of which radical 1980s music show?

32. Which collection of bear toys got their own Disney-produced cartoon show in the mid-1980s, and included the characters Cubbi, Gruffi, Sunni and Zummi?

33. Which member of the A-Team starred in a cartoon where he coached a team of teenage gymnasts who just happened to find and solve crimes wherever they competed?

34. What was the name of Keith Harris's lime green bird?

35. What was the name of Roland Rat's classy girlfriend: Glenis the Guinea Pig, Melinda the Mouse, Glenda the Gerbil, or Veronica the Vole?

36. Which one of the following comedy double acts regularly appeared on *The Saturday Gang*: the Chuckle Brothers, Lenny and Jerry, Cannon and Ball or Hale and Pace?

37. What was the real first name of the smaller member of the Krankies?

38. What show featured a Scottish lady with superhuman powers that she used to protect her town of Chisleton?

39. Which dance troupe replaced Legs and Co. on *Top of the Pops*: Ruby Flipper, Zoo or Rush and Bump?

40. Which ITV children's programme featured adults running a pirate TV show from a boiler room?

41. Can you name either of the boy and girl twins who lived in Cockleshell Bay?

42. Did Michael Rodd, Mark Curry, Mike Read or Mike Smith host *The Saturday Picture Show*, assisted by ex-Bucks Fizz singer, Cheryl Baker?

43. Which show about steam engines featured the Fat Controller and was narrated by the Beatle, Ringo Starr?

44. What was the title of the spin-off live action movie starring Dolph Lundgren as He-Man?

45. Which cartoon superhero ate a fruit to transform himself and had a crush on a newsreader called Fiona?

46. Can you name the children's drama show from the late eighties that featured a young Ant and Dec among its cast?

47. Chas, Nailbrush, Gillespie, Folly and Delilah all featured in which show about a plasticine character?

48. What was the name of Postman Pat's black and white cat?

49. Did Ringo Starr, Richard Briers, Peter Ustinov or Kenneth Williams provide the voice of cartoon character Dr Snuggles?

50. Was SuperTed's assistant called Lottie, Dotty or Spotty?

EVENTS

1. Who married Prince Andrew in 1986?

2. Which former Derby-winning horse was kidnapped in 1983?

3. In what year did the Live Aid concert take place?

4. Akihito became emperor of which country in 1989?

5. What was the name of the Tudor warship raised from the seabed in 1982?

6. Which Middle Eastern country lost its President, Prime Minister and 29 others in a 1981 bomb attack?

7. In which seaside town did an IRA bomb explode at the Conservative Party Conference?

8. What was the name of the Argentinian President who was removed from power shortly after the end of the Falklands War?

9. Along the coast of which American state did the Exxon Valdez spill millions of barrels of oil in 1989?

10. In 1988, three trains collided killing over 30 people at which London railway station?

11. In what year did the first Soviet Union's troops withdraw from Afghanistan?

12. The San Andreas Fault triggered a major earthquake in 1989 which killed over 270 people in which city?

13. What relation to the former leader of India was Rajiv Gandhi, who became India's Prime Minister in 1984?

14. Which country invaded Iran in 1980?

15. Over 1,000 protestors against apartheid were arrested when the South African rugby team toured England, New Zealand or Australia in 1981?

16. Which European country saw right-wing military forces take over the country's parliament?

17. In which year did McDonald's open its first branch in Moscow?

18. Which leader of the Soviet Union died in 1982?

19. What was the name of the trade union formed in Poland in 1980?

20. What was the name of the longest single-span suspension bridge in the world, completed in Britain in 1981?

21. Which space probe became the first to leave the solar system in 1983?

22. Which North African nation did US planes bomb in April 1986?

23. How many astronauts were killed when the space shuttle, Challenger, exploded?

24. In what year was the first British General Election of the 1980s?

25. In what year did a group of influential politicians break away from the Labour Party?

26. In which country did the Heysel Stadium disaster occur in 1985?

27. Who became leader of the Labour Party after James Callaghan?

28. Which one of the following British ships was not sunk during the Falklands War: MV *Atlantic Conveyor*, HMS *Antelope*, HMS *Sheffield* or HMS *York*?

29. Which Polish trade unionist was awarded the Nobel Peace Prize in 1983?

30. In what year did the British miners strike start?

31. The *Herald of Free Enterprise* sank in which sea in 1987?

32. The Strategic Defense Initiative (SDI) was known in the 1980s by what nickname?

33. Which country celebrated its bicentenary in 1988?

34. Which country passed the United States as the world's largest motor vehicle manufacturer in 1980?

35. Which club's fans were in the Heysel Stadium, along with Liverpool fans, in 1985?

36. With which other political party did the SDP form an alliance to fight the 1983 General Election?

37. In which country did a 1985 earthquake kill over 7,000 people?

38. A worldwide ban on ivory, tiger skin or eagle feathers occurred in 1989?

39. Which party won the 1987 British general election?

40. Who became President of France for the first time in 1981?

41. Which country's nuclear weapons were stored at Greenham Common provoking much protest?

42. In what year did the Brixton Riots occur?

43. Outside which London store did an IRA bomb explode in 1983, injuring 90 people and killing six?

44. In 1983, was the owner of the Heineken, Hofmeister or Carlsberg breweries released after a 14 million pound kidnap ransom was paid?

45. 520 people died in the worst air crash to date in which Asian country?

46. A fire at which English football ground killed over 50 people in 1985?

47. Shares in which British company went on sale in 1984, becoming the largest share issue in the world at that time?

48. What was the name of the warehouse which saw Britain's largest ever gold robbery in 1983?

49. PC Keith Blakelock was killed during riots in which part of London: Brixton, Tottenham or Harlesden?

50. Which country's wine was found to contain large amounts of antifreeze in 1985?

TELEVISION

1. What was the name of Bobby Ewing's wife in *Dallas*?

2. Which savage puppet show included a regular feature, The President's Brain is Missing, and spawned a chart single with 'The Chicken Song'?

3. What was the name of the sitcom which revolved around the lives of the Boswell family?

4. What sitcom, which ran from 1984 to 1992, featured the bar owned by Rene Artois which became a hideout for the French Resistance?

5. If you were watching Jim Hacker MP struggling with his civil servants, which sitcom were you viewing?

6. Which one of the following musicians and singers did not make a guest appearance in *Miami Vice*: Little Richard, Barbera Streisand, Bono, James Brown or Phil Collins?

7. If you were watching Sandy Richardson in a wheelchair talking to chef Shughie McFee, which soap were you viewing?

8. Who played the last incarnation of Dr Who in the eighties: Colin Baker, Peter Davidson or Sylvester McCoy?

9. If you were watching the goings on in Ramsay Street in the late eighties, what soap were you tuning into?

10. What was the name of the wife of John Walton and the mother of John Boy Walton?

11. What was the name of the club in which *Minder's* Arthur Daley spent much of his time being served drinks by Dave?

12. Which US sitcom featured Danny Devito as Louie DePalma raging away at his employees from the safety of his caged office?

13. Which sitcom featured actor Karl Howman playing a cheeky cockney painter and decorator?

14. What was the name of the lead character in the comedy *The New Statesman*?

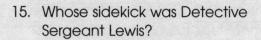

15. Whose sidekick was Detective Sergeant Lewis?

16. In *Dynasty*, what was the name of the company Alexis took over after her husband's death, to become Blake Carrington's arch-business rival?

17. Can you name all four of Jock Ewing's sons?

18. What was the name of the ITV Granada show planned as a weekend accompaniment to *Coronation Street* and set in a Manchester street market?

19. Which one of the *Red Dwarf* cast was a hologram?

20. Which English actor played the lead in *The Equalizer*. John Thaw, Edward Woodward, Ian Ogilvy or Richard Harris?

21. Which drama show, about the lives of a group of firefighters know as the Blue Watch, made its debut as a serial in 1988?

22. Which one of the following was not a guest star in *Roseanne*: Jerry Springer, Joanna Lumley, George Clooney, Ruby Wax or Tony Curtis?

23. Who was the matriarchal head of the Ewing family?

24. What was the surname of the cleaner wife and the dustman husband found in *Coronation Street*?

25. In *Auf Wiedersehen, Pet*, which two of the following was not a Geordie: Oz, Moxy, Neville, Dennis or Barry?

26. Which show featured the powerful 'Knight Industries Two Thousand' car?

27. Which actor played Dr Who at the very start of the 1980s?

28. Which sitcom charted the ebbing and flowing romance between Penny and Vince, the latter played by Paul Nicholas?

29. Which American show featured stuntman and bounty hunter, Colt Seavers, played by ex-*Six Million Dollar Man* actor, Lee Majors?

30. What was the name of Roseanne's policewoman sister?

31. *Gregory's Girl* actress and Altered Images singer, Clare Grogan, played Kochanski in which popular space-based sitcom?

32. Which comedy drama about an ageing Scottish rock 'n' roll band called the Majestics, featured Emma Thompson and Robbie Coltrane?

33. Which British sitcom family lived at number 368 Nelson Mandela House?

34. Was *The Wonder Years, All in the Family* or *Married with Children* a story focusing on a boy called Kevin Arnold?

35. Who hosted the first series of *Blind Date* in 1985?

36. Joanna Lumley, and which former *Man from U.N.C.L.E.* actor, starred in *Sapphire and Steel*?

37. Which satire of American daytime dramas was the story of two sisters, Jessica Tate and Mary Campbell, and their ridiculously complicated family lives?

38. Which comedy show featured a pet hamster called SPG and featured a punk, a hippie, a student who idolised Cliff Richard and Mike the Cool Person?

39. Which comedy double act was famous for their two gangster-style bouncers, Ron and Ron?

40. Which short-lived but much-remembered outlandish US show featured Dr Jonathan Chase who was capable of turning into a range of different creatures?

41. Who was at the helm of the Enterprise when *Star Trek: The Next Generation* returned to screens in the late 1980s?

42. Which BBC news journalist's reports of the suffering in Ethiopia moved a nation, and inspired Bob Geldof to start Live Aid?

43. What was the name of the character who was the chief civil service advisor to Jim Hacker in both *Yes, Minister* and *Yes, Prime Minister*?

44. Who was the host of the popular late eighties quiz show *Strike it Lucky*?

45. Which quiz show featured Bob Monkhouse, Max Bygraves and Les Dennis as the hosts at different times during the 1980s?

46. In which year was *Crossroads* axed for the first time?

47. Can you name the ITV newsreader who was the subject of the *Not the Nine O'Clock News* team's song, 'Oh, Reggie'?

48. If you were watching two 'good ol' boys' evading Sheriff Rosco P. Coltrane, what show were you viewing?

49. Which former sports presenter was one of the two hosts of BBC's *Breakfast Time*?

50. In which year did the Children in Need appeal first appear?

MUSIC

1. Whose eighties albums included: *Hot Space*, *The Works* and *The Miracle*?

2. 'Rise' was a hit for which band fronted by the former Sex Pistol, John Lydon?

3. Which group featured the frontman David Bryne?

4. What was the name of the Paul Simon album which featured African musicians and rhythms?

5. Which singer sang with the Miami Sound Machine on tracks like 'Dr Beat'?

6. Whose first solo album was called *Faith*?

7. In which year of the eighties would you find 'Footloose', 'Karma Chameleon' and 'When Doves Cry' riding high in the singles charts?

8. Which future film star was the Fresh Prince in the rap act DJ Jazzy Jeff and the Fresh Prince?

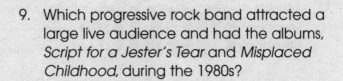

9. Which progressive rock band attracted a large live audience and had the albums, *Script for a Jester's Tear* and *Misplaced Childhood*, during the 1980s?

10. Which ska band's members formed the Fine Young Cannibals: the Selecter, the Specials or the Beat?

11. Which a cappella band had a hit with the Yazoo track 'Only You'?

12. Who had a major dance hit with the track 'Nineteen': Paul Hardcastle, Tone Loc or Adamski?

13. Which group was the only act to appear on both the original Band Aid and the Band Aid II charity singles?

14. A video, for which Queen single, featured the band in drag parading around a house?

15. Which group had a number one single with 'Perfect' and featured Eddi Reader as the lead singer?

16. Which band was fronted by Robert Smith and had records including 'Charlotte Sometimes'?

17. *Master of Puppets* was a 1988 album by Marillion, Metallica, Mike and the Mechanics, or Sonic Youth?

18. In which year did the Police split-up: 1980, 1984 or 1988?

19. Which band would you be watching if it contained Chas Smash?

20. UB40 had a hit with `Red, Red Wine' in the mid-1980s: did Bunny Wailer, Bob Marley, Peter Tosh or Neil Diamond write the song?

21. Which was the only band of the 1980s to have their first three single releases reach number one?

22. Philip Bailey from Earth Wind and Fire teamed up with which member of Genesis for a major hit with `Easy Lover'?

23. Diana Ross's `Chain Reaction' was written and produced by Stock, Aitken and Waterman, the Bee Gees or Billy Ocean?

24. Which heavy rock guitarist provided the solo for Michael Jackson's `Beat it'?

25. Doctor and the Medics had one major hit single. What was it called?

26. What was the name of the band featuring Jimmy Sommerville which formed after Bronski Beat?

27. What was the name of U2's second album, released in 1981?

28. Which band, featuring the future Fatboy Slim, had a 1986 number one with 'Caravan of Love'?

29. M/A/R/R/S had a major late eighties dance hit with 'Killer', 'Pump Up the Volume' or 'Dub Be Good to Me'?

30. Bros, Swing out Sister or Nik Kershaw had a hit with 'I Owe You Nothing'?

31. What was the name of the two former Wham backing singers who had chart success in 1987: Mel and Kim, Salt 'n' Peppa, or Pepsi and Shirlie?

32. The Toy Dolls had a novelty hit in the eighties with a song about what animal?

33. Who was 'Big Legee' according to Haysi Fantayzee?

34. 'Boxer Beat' was an early eighties hit for the Jo Boxers, the Assembly, Then Jerico or the Fun Boy Three?

35. In what year did Marvin Gaye, Jackie Wilson and Count Basie all die?

36. Which band, formed in 1980 by the Sex Pistols' manager, featured a 14 year old girl as lead singer and later had a hit with 'Wild in the Country'?

37. Which song about dropping an atomic bomb became a big hit for OMD?

38. Steve Strange fronted: Landscape, A Flock of Seagulls, Visage or Alphaville?

39. Big Audio Dynamite were the brainchild of a former member of the Cure, Human League, the Clash or Devo?

40. Whose debut LP had his name at the end of the title: *Introducing the Hardline According to...*?

41. Which one of the following acts was not a guest on *The Tube's* final show: the Cure, Tina Turner, Echo and the Bunnymen or U2?

42. Which year saw the lead singer of AC/DC die, Cliff Richard awarded an MBE and the Jam's album, *Sound Affects,* released?

43. Which U2 album featured 'Pride (In the Name of Love)'?

44. In which year did Bob Geldof receive a honorary knighthood for his charity efforts?

45. Can you name two out of the three Goss brothers who first formed Bros?

46. What year was dubbed 'Acid House's Summer of Love'?

47. The power ballad 'Just Died in Your Arms Tonight' was a major hit for Berlin, Cutting Crew, Jim Diamond or Foreigner?

48. Which band played their first live gig in April 1980 and released their debut single, 'Radio Free Europe', a short time later?

49. Which futurist singer collaborated with Giorgio Moroder on the hit 'Together in Electric Dreams'?

50. Which year were the following singles among the biggest sellers: 'I Wanna Dance With Somebody', 'You Win Again' and 'Nothing's Gonna Stop Us Now'?

FILMS AND FILM STARS

1. In which 1989 film did Meg Ryan memorably act out an orgasm in a diner?

2. Who played Al Capone in the film *The Untouchables*?

3. Which film featured two sunglasses and suit-wearing musicians on a 'mission from God'?

4. *Private Benjamin* starred Jane Fonda, Meryl Streep, Demi Moore, Goldie Hawn or Jodie Foster?

5. Which movie character of the eighties inspired millions of kids to stick out a finger and say 'phone home'?

6. Which classic horror film featured a writer staying with his wife and child at the Overlook Hotel and gradually going insane?

7. Which Oscar winning film tells the tale of Sydney Schanberg, a journalist covering the Cambodian War?

8. Which film featured a demented Christopher Lloyd, a perplexed Michael J. Fox and a time-travelling Delorean car for the first time?

9. Which 1986 movie featured Ducky Dale who had a crush on Andie Walsh who, in turn, falls for rich kid, Blane McDonough?

10. Who played bass guitar in the mythical band Spinal Tap?

11. What was the name of the heartwarming film about alien powers rejuvenating the inhabitants of an old peoples' home?

12. Which Tim Burton film featured Michael Keaton as a demonic force: Beetlejuice, Pee Wee's Big Adventure or Batman?

13. Which Oscar winning drama featured Jack Nicholson as a retired astronaut called Garrett Breedlove?

14. Peter Falk (Columbo), Christopher Guest (Spinal Tap guitarist), Billy Crystal and Peter Cook all starred in which comedy fairy tale?

15. Which chilling special effects-driven film featured the eerie and unfriendly Slaughtered Lamb pub?

16. 1984 saw the third and, for many, the finest Muppet movie. What was it called?

17. *Desperately Seeking Susan* launched the acting career of which female pop singer?

18. In which 1980s movie did Tom Cruise play a wheelchair-bound Vietnam veteran?

19. What was the name of Charlie Sheen's character in the film *Wall Street*: Gordon Gecko, Bud Fox or Harry Costello?

20. Which Australian actor found fleeting film stardom as Michael J. Dundee?

21. Which one of the following Brat Pack stars, was not in *St Elmo's Fire*: Judd Nelson, Ally Sheedy, Molly Ringwald, Demi Moore or Rob Lowe?

22. Which actor was found in all the following eighties movies: *Trading Places, The Blues Brothers* and *Ghostbusters*?

23. Michael Douglas has an affair with which actress's character, who returns to haunt him in *Fatal Attraction*?

24. Which romantic drama featured trainee Navy pilot, Zack Mayo, wrestling with his past and his heart?

25. Which 1987 romantic film re-launched Cher's career as an actress?

26. The mermaid in *Splash* was named after which part of New York: Brooklyn, Queens, Madison or Yonkers?

27. Which 1980 film adaptation of a Clive Cussler novel about a sunken ship, starred Jason Robards and Alec Guinness?

28. Which comedy featured Dudley Moore and Sir John Gielgud as his butler?

29. Which 1982 epic won eight Oscars and starred: John Mills, Martin Sheen, Sir John Gielgud and Ben Kingsley?

30. Which British film about athletes in the 1920s, swept the Oscars in 1981?

31. Which actor appeared in *Superman IV, Reds, Mississippi Burning* and *Hoosiers*?

32. Which 1980 comedy about women taking charge starred Dolly Parton, Lily Tomlin and Jane Fonda?

33. Which actor starred in both *Airplane* films and the 1988 comedy, *Naked Gun*?

34. Which two of the following eighties films did not feature Jeanette Charles playing Queen Elizabeth II: *Naked Gun, National Lampoon's European Vacation, Airplane* or *Spies Like Us*?

35. Which film told the tale of an actor forced to cross-dress to obtain a lead role?

36. Christopher Guest (Nigel Tufnell in Spinal Tap), married Jamie Lee Curtis, Deborah Winger or Rosanna Arquette in the 1980s?

37. Which pair of brothers played pianists in the film *The Fabulous Baker Boys*?

38. Which comedy film featured the Duke brothers and Louis Winthop III, the latter played by Dan Ackroyd?

39. Which actor starred in the following: *Brubaker, Out of Africa* and *Legal Eagles*?

40. What 1987 film about a TV news team starred William Hurt and Holly Hunter?

41. Which one of the following musicians did not feature in *The Blues Brothers*: Ray Charles, B.B. King or James Brown?

42. Which two of the following appeared in Rocky III: Hulk Hogan, Mr T or O.J. Simpson?

43. What was the name of the 1983 sequel to the seventies film *Saturday Night Fever*?

44. Which actress played roles in *Terms of Endearment, An Officer and a Gentleman* and *Legal Eagles*?

45. Which actress starred in *Wall Street, Blade Runner, Steel Magnolias* and *Splash*?

46. Which actor was found in all the following eighties movies: *Little Shop of Horrors, Ghostbusters, Caddy Shack* and *Stripes*?

47. Which 1989 Woody Allen film told the story of an optician, played by Martin Landau, who conducts a long affair?

48. Which 1988 action blockbuster featured Alan Rickman as villain Hans Gruber?

49. Who won a Best Actor Oscar for his portrayal of a gay prisoner in the 1985 movie *Kiss of the Spider Woman*?

50. What film featured a strange furry creature given as a pet, that soon breeds and goes out of control?

SCIENCE AND TECHNOLOGY

1. In what year was the first space shuttle launched into space?

2. What new music format was developed by Phillips and Sony in the early 1980s?

3. What celestial body could be viewed from earth in 1986?

4. What were the Oric, Dragon 32 and the Atmos?

5. What form of cosmetic surgery was first introduced in 1982?

6. What sort of device was Jason Jr: an underwater robot, a space camera or a pilotless plane?

7. What sort of pollution generated in the northern European nations caused devastation of forests and lakes in Scandinavia during the 1980s?

8. In what year was the first video camcorder introduced?

9. American company, 3M, introduced what handy item of stationery in 1981?

10. Was Challenger, Columbia, Enterprise or Spirit the first space shuttle to make a space flight?

11. What atmospheric problem was discovered in 1985?

12. In which country were the principles of genetic fingerprinting discovered in 1985?

13. In what year was the Apple Macintosh introduced to the public?

14. British chemist, Sir Harry Kroto, discovered a new form of carbon, gold, or atomic particles in the 1980s?

15. What music compression software was first patented in Germany, in 1989?

16. Computer engineer and visionary, Jaron Lanier, coined which computing term in 1983?

17. Which company produced the first disposable camera in 1986?

18. What disposable form of eyewear was invented in 1987?

19. Ray Fuller invented which drug in 1987: Prozac, Ecstacy or Viagra?

20. Which computer operating system was first released in 1985?

21. Was synthetic skin invented in 1983, 1986 or 1989?

22. Which country sent two space probes to fly past Halley's Comet in 1985?

23. What was the name of the space probe that sent back images of Saturn and its moons in 1980?

24. Was Centipede, Pacman or Defender the first video arcade game designed by a woman?

25. Which novel camera film format was introduced in 1982: APS, 35mm or Kodak disc film?

26. Which new digital recording format was introduced in 1986?

27. In 1986, Voyager 2 sent back images of which distant planet?

28. Which company produced their first portable CD player in 1988?

29. What was the name of the 1988 book written by scientist Stephen Hawking?

30. Which well-known magazine was the first to put a hologram on its cover in 1984?

31. The first wristwatch-TV went on sale in 1984, 1986 or 1988?

32. What did Sally Ride become the first American woman to do in 1983?

33. Over which continent was the hole in the ozone layer discovered in the mid-1980s?

34. What was the name of the space station launched in 1986 by the Soviet Union?

35. What was used to convict criminals for the first time in 1987?

36. What was the name of Sinclair's first colour home computer: the ZX81, the Sinclair QL, ZX82 or the Spectrum?

37. What system of program storage did the Amstrad CPC464 home computer use: a 5.25 inch floppy disk, a memory card or a cassette tape?

38. Which sunken ship was discovered by robot technology in 1985?

39. How many moons of Saturn did the Voyager 2 space probe discover in the early 1980s?

40. Tim Berners-Lee was a major figure in developing what form of computer-based communication in the 1980s?

41. How many IBM PCs were sold in 1981: 25,000, 250,000 or 2.5 million?

42. Which country accused the United States of causing environmental damage in 1982?

43. William Gibson's 1984 novel, *Neuromancer*, coined the term: 'the internet', 'cyber-space' or 'virtual reality'?

44. Which Microsoft computer program was first introduced in 1987: Word, Excel, Internet Explorer or Paint?

45. What object did *Time* magazine name Machine of the Year in 1982?

46. Which Apple computer was the first to feature a computer mouse: the Apple II, the Lisa or the Maz 1?

47. Which substances were the subject of the 1987 Montreal Accords which aimed to ban them by 2000?

48. What mechanical body part was first successfully transplanted in 1982?

49. Did Dell, Compaq, Atari or Tandy produce the first practical, battery-powered notebook computer in 1989?

50. What sort of aircraft was the Lockheed F117A which first flew in the early 1980s: a stealth fighter, a stealth bomber, a new supersonic airliner or a prototype of the world's largest airliner?

ANSWERS

QUIZ 1

KIDS' TELEUISION

1. He-Man
2. Timmy Mallett
3. Errol
4. Penfold
5. Ziggy Greaves
6. *Saturday Superstore*
7. *Transformers*
8. *Runaround*
9. *Crackerjack*
10. *Happy Days*

11. Baron Silas Greenback
12. *Fraggle Rock*
13. Bananaman
14. *Beat the Teacher*
15. *Postman Pat*
16. *Grange Hill*
17. *Dungeons and Dragons*
18. *Button Moon*
19. Mike Read
20. Gordon

21. Pink
22. Skeletor
23. *The Adventure Game*
24. Mumm-Ra
25. *SuperTed*
26. *The A-Team*

27. BBC Micro
28. *Byker Grove*
29. Battlecat
30. Dr Snuggles

31. Lion-O
32. Cliff Huxtable
33. Terrahawks
34. *The Trap Door*
35. *Different Strokes*
36. *Press Gang*
37. She-Ra
38. *The Wide Awake Club*
39. *Dogtanian and the Three Muskehounds*
40. *Dungeons and Dragons*

41. The Fonz
42. BBC1
43. The Smurfs
44. *Hartbeat*
45. Terrahawks
46. Zammo (Samuel Maguire)
47. Mike Read
48. Mrs Goggins
49. Gary Crowley
50. John 'Hannibal' Smith

QUIZ 2

CELEBRITIES

1. 1981
2. John Lennon
3. Joan Collins
4. John Belushi
5. Cecil Parkinson
6. Six
7. Prince Harry
8. Peter Sellers
9. Ronald Reagan
10. Ronald Reagan

11. Jimmy Carter
12. Ruth Lawrence
13. Soviet Union
14. Peter Sutcliffe
15. Surrogate mother
16. Princess Grace of Monaco
17. Israel
18. John McCarthy
19. Jeffrey Archer
20. Prince William

21. Contraception
22. Michael Fagan
23. George Bush
24. Salman Rushdie
25. Richard Branson

26. Desmond Tutu
27. 1986
28. Bill Rogers, Shirley Williams, Roy Jenkins, David Owen
29. Rudolf Hess
30. Cynthia Payne

31. Margaret Thatcher
32. The Nobel Peace Prize
33. Japan
34. Pope John Paul II
35. 17 men
36. AIDS
37. Yul Brynner
38. 19
39. Gary Kasparov
40. Prince Philip

41. Edwina Currie
42. Clint Eastwood
43. Vice President
44. Lester Piggott
45. Hungerford
46. Pakistan
47. Terry Waite
48. Ferdinand Marcos
49. Milli Vanilli
50. John Lennon

FUN AND GAMES

1. Six
2. Barbie
3. Raleigh Grifter
4. Lego
5. Four
6. Rubik's Cube
7. *Ghostbusters*
8. *The Secret Diary of Adrian Mole Aged 13 $\frac{3}{4}$*
9. A dog
10. The Sinclair ZX81

11. Cabbage Patch Kids
12. Raleigh
13. Care Bears
14. Lo-lo Ball
15. Transformers
16. Tetris
17. Frogger
18. Brown
19. Pictionary
20. A La Carte Kitchen

21. Donkey Kong Jr
22. Cabbage Patch Kid
23. Pacman
24. White
25. A small portable music synthesizer

26. My Little Pony
27. The Sinclair Spectrum
28. Glow Worm
29. Raphael, Leonardo, Donatello and Michelangelo
30. Transformers

31. False
32. He-Man
33. Hulk Hogan
34. 16 (4 x 4 square)
35. Smurfette
36. Matey
37. Cabbage Patch Dolls
38. Care Bears
39. Commodore
40. Long-haired footballers

41. Nintendo Gameboy
42. Panini
43. Action Man
44. Sinclair Spectrum
45. True
46. Scruples
47. Yellow
48. Scalextric
49. Retractable stabilizers
50. My Little Pony

QUIZ 4

TELEVISION

1. *Cheers*
2. *To the Manor Born*
3. J.R. Ewing
4. *Last of the Summer Wine*
5. Yellow
6. Pierce Brosnan
7. Alexei Sayle
8. *M.A.S.H.*
9. *Minder*
10. *Blackadder*

11. *Two's Company*
12. *Red Dwarf*
13. *Hill Street Blues*
14. *Dynasty*
15. Les Dawson
16. *The Young Ones*
17. The Blue Moon Agency
18. Paul Daniels
19. *The Colbys*
20. Cliff Barnes

21. Inspector Morse
22. Jim Rockford
23. Den and Angie Watts
24. Sam Malone
25. The *Hitchhiker's Guide to the Galaxy*

26. *Hart to Hart*
27. London taxi driver
28. *Auf Wiedersehen, Pet*
29. Tom Cruise
30. Channel 4

31. Becky and Darlene
32. *Blake's Seven*
33. *Airwolf*
34. Ricardo Tubbs
35. Third
36. *Cagney and Lacey*
37. Jessica Fletcher
38. *Not the Nine O'Clock News*
39. Krystle
40. *Only When I Laugh*

41. Freeway
42. Ernie 'Coach' Pantuso
43. Boycie
44. *Juliet Bravo*
45. Four
46. Kristin Barnes
47. *Triangle*
48. Zeb and Esther
49. *Open All Hours*
50. Captain Darling

QUIZ 5

MUSIC

1. 99
2. Band Aid
3. Kraftwerk
4. De La Soul
5. ABC
6. Vince Clark
7. The Young Ones
8. Roland Gift
9. Def Leppard
10. Madness

11. Phil Collins
12. Sade
13. Sinitta
14. Captain Sensible
15. Survivor
16. 'Tainted Love'
17. 'Two Tribes'
18. Aztec Camera
19. 'Snooker Loopy'
20. *Beverley Hills Cop*

21. Yazz
22. Michael Jackson
23. *Hysteria*
24. Pink Floyd
25. 'Let it Be'
26. Falco

27. Black Box
28. *Brothers in Arms*
29. Tears for Fears
30. 'Do They Know it's Christmas Time?'

31. Phil Collins
32. 'Atomic'
33. Electric Light Orchestra (E.L.O.)
34. ABBA
35. *M.A.S.H.*
36. Haircut One Hundred
37. St Winifred's
38. Buck's Fizz
39. 'Stand and Deliver'
40. Midge Ure

41. Queen
42. Goombay Dance Band
43. Julio Inglesias
44. 'The Edge of Heaven'
45. Human League
46. Yazoo
47. 'The Winner Takes it All'
48. 'We are the World'
49. USA for Africa
50. Talking Heads

QUIZ 6

SPORT

1. South Korea
2. Ben Johnson
3. Daley Thomson
4. Jayne Torvill and Christopher Dean
5. Ipswich Town
6. Bill Werbeniuk
7. Darts
8. Sebastian Coe
9. David Gower
10. Aston Villa

11. Thomas Hearns
12. Three
13. Dundee United
14. 1987
15. Manchester United
16. Wade Dooley
17. Peter Shilton
18. Number 10
19. Aberdeen
20. 1984

21. Jack Nicklaus
22. Moscow
23. Bob Willis
24. Alain Prost

25. French
26. Lake Placid
27. Fatima Whitbread
28. Alan Border
29. Wimbledon
30. Jonathan Davies

31. Ray Reardon
32. Arsenal
33. Eric Bristow
34. Pole-vault
35. Sarajevo
36. Keke Rosberg
37. Coventry City
38. Duncan Goodhew
39. Spain
40. Ian Botham

41. Los Angeles
42. Vijay Armitraj
43. West Germany
44. Heptathlon
45. Linford Christie
46. Serge Blanco
47. Robin Cousins
48. Steve Davis
49. England
50. 1985

QUIZ 7

FILMS AND FILM STARS

1. *Top Gun*
2. *Indiana Jones and the Raiders of the Lost Ark*
3. *Rain Man*
4. *Lethal Weapon*
5. *This is Spinal Tap*
6. *Back to the Future*
7. *Airplane*
8. Tom Cruise
9. Gene Hackman
10. *The Empire Strikes Back*

11. *Aliens*
12. *An Officer and a Gentleman*
13. Nicole Kidman
14. Brooke Shields
15. Don Johnson
16. *E.T.*
17. Michael Keaton
18. John Rambo
19. *Wall Street*
20. *Do the Right Thing*

21. *Beetlejuice*
22. *Raging Bull*
23. *On Golden Pond*
24. *Dead Poets' Society*

25. *Ted Danson*
26. *Dirty Dancing*
27. *Hannah and her Sisters*
28. *Gregory's Girl*
29. Eddie Murphy
30. Jodie Foster

31. Nicholas Cage
32. *Dangerous Liaisons*
33. *Platoon*
34. The Ark of the Covenant
35. *Trading Places*
36. *When Harry Met Sally*
37. Tom Hanks
38. Whoopi Goldberg
39. Gene Hackman
40. *Wall Street*

41. *Airplane*
42. *Beverley Hills Cop*
43. *The Terminator*
44. *Ferris Bueller's Day Off*
45. Kim Basinger
46. *Beetlejuice*
47. *The Breakfast Club*
48. Michelle Pfeiffer
49. Diane Keaton
50. *This is Spinal Tap*

QUIZ 8

ARTS AND ENTERTAINMENT

1. Salman Rushdie
2. Van Gogh
3. *Starlight Express*
4. William Golding
5. Peter Wright
6. Douglas Adams
   (*The Hitchhiker's Guide
   to the Galaxy*)
7. Hitler's Diaries
8. 1986
9. China
10. Egyptian

11. The Barbican
12. Julian Barnes
13. New York
14. Salvador Dali
15. Goblins
16. Mary Whitehouse
17. *A Question of Honour*
18. *Amadeus*
19. *Sweeney Todd*
20. The Hacienda

21. Stephen King
22. John Updike
23. *Aspects of Love*
24. *Midnight's Children*
25. Peter Carey

26. *The Restaurant at the
    End of the Universe*
27. The Louvre
28. The Cavern
29. Roddy Doyle
30. The Comedy Store

31. *The Remains of the Day*
32. Prince Charles
33. Kingsley Amis
34. *Superfudge*
35. *Schindler's Ark*
36. Lloyd's Building
37. Iris Murdoch
38. *The Phantom of the
    Opera*
39. Ted Hughes
40. *Glengarry Glen Ross*

41. Norman Mailer
42. *Cats*
43. Alice Walker
44. Dennis Potter
45. Tom Clancy
46. John Updike
47. Carl Sagan
48. 1980
49. Steve Bell
50. Mike Myers

EVENTS

1. The Berlin Wall
2. Pope John Paul II
3. Delorean
4. Tito
5. Argentina
6. The Soviet Union
7. Scotland
8. Kings Cross
9. Rhodesia
10. Mount St Helens

11. Washington
12. Over five years
13. 1987
14. 14 miles
15. The Italian parliament
16. Toxteth
17. Challenger
18. Hampton Court
19. 1987
20. Beirut

21. General Belgrano
22. The Iran-Iraq War
23. Grenada
24. Cory Aquino
25. Korean Airlines

26. Lebanon
27. Tiananmen
28. Glasnost
29. Robert Mugabe
30. Iran

31. 1981
32. Egypt
33. 1982
34. The Labour Party
35. New York
36. Libyan
37. Indira Gandhi
38. Konstantin Chernenko
39. Ronald Reagan
40. Burma

41. Neil Kinnock
42. 45 nations
43. Sweden
44. 1989
45. 1986
46. Vietnam
47. George Bush
48. Michael Dukakis
49. Moscow (Red Square)
50. Statue of Liberty

QUIZ 10

TELEVISION

1. *Magnum P.I.*
2. *Crossroads*
3. *T.J. Hooker*
4. *Play Your Cards Right*
5. Holly
6. *Dempsey and Makepeace*
7. *Boys from the Black Stuff*
8. Dead at Thirty
9. Los Angeles
10. *Roseanne*

11. 1985
12. Fallon, Steven, Adam and Amanda
13. *Lovejoy*
14. *The Bill*
15. *Hill Street Blues*
16. Maddy Hayes
17. Mickey Pearce
18. *St Elsewhere*
19. Kevin Turvey
20. Loadsamoney

21. Kenny Everett
22. *Taxi*
23. *Bullseye*
24. Trigger
25. *Blockbusters*
26. Neil, Rick, Mike and Vyvyan

27. Southfork
28. Australia
29. Lord Flashheart
30. *Knot's Landing*

31. *Duty Free*
32. Russ Abbott
33. Jim Rockford
34. *Brookside*
35. Francis 'Ponch' Poncherello and Jonathan Baker
36. Lord Snot, Kendal Mintcake, Lord Monty and Miss Money-Sterling
37. Elizabeth
38. *Lovejoy*
39. *Mork and Mindy*
40. *3-2-1*

41. *Neighbours*
42. *Bergerac*
43. David Addison
44. *Roseanne*, D.J.
45. Jim Carver
46. Nine
47. Nursie and Lord Melchett
48. Scullion
49. Bomber
50. *Dear John*

LIFE

1. Yuppies
2. Breville
3. London
4. Green
5. O-Levels
6. The Channel Tunnel
7. Ikea
8. Laker Airways
9. Arthur Scargill
10. 1986

11. £399
12. The compact disc
13. The Poll Tax
14. The filofax
15. 1986
16. London Docklands
17. Lands' End
18. 1982
19. *Countdown*
20. 1985

21. CNN
22. 5,4,3,2,1
23. The sixpence (2.5p)
24. The compact disc
25. 1983

26. Petrol
27. The F-Plan diet
28. 1983
29. 1987
30. London

31. Bobby Sands
32. St Paul's Cathedral
33. Pot Noodle
34. Ken Livingstone
35. *Today*
36. The Docklands
37. Scotland
38. Michael Jackson
39. 1988
40. *The Independent*

41. Cadbury's Creme Eggs
42. Mark Allen
43. Break dancing
44. Sloan Rangers
45. Cider, Cola
46. The pump dispenser
47. Blue
48. The breakfast bar
49. Val-speak
50. 1987

QUIZ 12

MUSIC

1. Dexy's Midnight Runners
2. Martha and the Muffins
3. 'Reet Petite'
4. *Miami Vice*
5. Birmingham
6. The Teardrop Explodes
7. Grandmaster Flash and the Furious Five
8. Limahl
9. Sheena Easton
10. Lisa Stansfield

11. Three
12. The Smiths
13. Cyndi Lauper
14. Europe
15. 'Take My Breath Away'
16. Neil (Nigel Planer)
17. 'Vienna'
18. Wham
19. 'If I Was'
20. Billy Idol

21. Half Man, Half Biscuit
22. The Bangles
23. Duran Duran
24. The Style Council
25. Madonna
26. Roxy Music

27. Wet, Wet, Wet
28. Human League
29. New Order
30. The Undertones

31. Norwegian
32. Happy Mondays
33. *Strangeways Here We Come*
34. Run DMC
35. Air Supply
36. Neneh Cherry
37. Elvis Costello
38. The The
39. Bon Jovi
40. Rick Astley

41. Stock, Aitken and Waterman
42. Z. Z. Top
43. Iron Maiden
44. David Lee Roth
45. Jim Kerr
46. Jane Fonda
47. Curiosity Killed the Cat
48. The Beastie Boys
49. 1987
50. *The Final Cut* and *A Momentary Lapse of Reason*

ADVERTISING

1. Paul Hogan
2. Kia-Ora
3. TSB
4. Topic
5. British Telecom
6. Um Bongo
7. J.R. Hartley
8. British Gas
9. Tetleys
10. Lorraine Chase

11. Campari
12. British Telecom
13. British Airways
14. Anthony Head
15. Alan Whicker
16. 'I Heard it Through the Grapevine'
17. Toshiba
18. Holsten Pils
19. Cornetto
20. British Gas

21. The Ribenaberries
22. Paxo
23. Lenny Henry
24. 2000
25. Maureen Lipman

26. The *Independent*
27. Carling Black Label
28. Nike
29. Run DMC
30. Creature Comforts

31. Impulse
32. A ballet
33. *Fly Fishing*
34. George
35. Castlemaine XXXX
36. Toothbrushes
37. Milton Keynes
38. Bird's Eye
39. Sekonda watches
40. Monster Munch

41. Michael Jackson
42. Access
43. Vorsprung Durch Technik
44. Cadbury's Finger of Fudge
45. The Leeds
46. Uniroyal
47. Sinclair ZX81
48. Bandit
49. Fresca
50. Outer Spacers

QUIZ 14

FASHION AND FADS

1. The Body Shop
2. *Fame*
3. Moon Boots
4. Nike
5. Next
6. Shaving
7. Jellies
8. Chinos
9. Goth
10. Michael Jackson

11. The Mullet
12. The Miami Vice look
13. Garfield
14. Mark Knopfler
15. A type of trainer with velcro pockets
16. Madonna
17. Swatch
18. Aviators
19. Pineapple Dance Studio
20. Bolero jacket

21. Katherine Hamnett
22. Vivienne Westwood
23. Baggy and metallic jeans
24. Crimping
25. Princess Diana
26. Emanuel
27. Hugo Boss

28. Lacoste
29. *Flashdance, Footloose* and *Fame*
30. Jane Fonda

31. Frankie Goes to Hollywood
32. Benetton
33. Pedal Pushers
34. Ra-ra skirts
35. Cycling shorts
36. Power suits with padded shoulders
37. *Magnum PI*
38. Ralph Lauren
39. Belgium
40. Menswear (1984), interior furnishings (1985), children's wear (1987)

41. On your head
42. Madonna
43. True
44. The smiley face
45. Barbour
46. Manchester
47. Adam Ant
48. Shell suit
49. Ceroc
50. A small braided piece of hair

QUIZ 15

SPORT

1. Zola Budd
2. Eric Bristow
3. England
4. Diego Maradona
5. Boris Becker
6. Dennis Taylor
7. Bryan Robson
8. Jo Durie
9. Liverpool
10. John Lowe

11. Aston Villa
12. Niki Lauda
13. Marvin Hagler
14. Martina Navratilova
15. Poland
16. Hockey
17. Quarter finals
18. A plastic pitch
19. New Zealand
20. Nelson Piquet

21. Greg Louganis
22. Paraguay
23. Wales
24. Carl Lewis
25. Kenny Dalglish

26. Marathon
27. Matchroom
28. 1980
29. Bryan Robson
30. Nigel Mansell

31. *Bolero* by Ravel
32. Peter Fleming
33. Chris Broad
34. Matt Biondi
35. Tennis
36. Spain, West Germany
37. Liverpool
38. Javed Miandad
39. Pat Cash
40. Ron Greenwood

41. Alain Prost
42. Kevin Keegan
43. Cliff Thorburn
44. St Mirren
45. Alan Wells
46. Dino Zoff
47. West Germany
48. Bill Werbeniuk
49. Everton
50. Bjorn Borg

QUIZ 16

KIDS' TELEVISION

1. *Pigeon Street*
2. His left
3. *Different Strokes*
4. Rolf Harris
5. *Inspector Gadget*
6. Arthur Fonzarelli
7. *T-Bag*
8. Keith Chegwin
   (*Cheggars Plays Pop*)
9. *The Adventure Game*
10. *We are the Champions*

11. Phillip Schofield
12. Trevor Cleaver, Pogo
    Patterson
13. Pansy Pig, Ted Tortoise,
    Chris Rabbit
14. South America
15. *Tucker's Luck*
16. *Knightmare*
17. Scrappy-Do
18. *The A-Team*
19. *Finders Keepers*
20. Dangermouse

21. *Challenge of the GoBots*
22. *The Flumps*
23. False (the actor played
    the voice of Papa Smurf
    and Scooby-Do)
24. She-Ra

25. Count Duckula
26. *Fireball XL5*
27. *Around the World with
    Willy Fogg*
28. Mightius
29. Dr Snuggles
30. The Ewoks

31. *The Tube*
32. The Gummi Bears
33. Orville
34. True
35. Glenis the Guinea Pig
36. Hale and Pace
37. Jeanette
38. *Supergran*
39. Zoo
40. *CBTV*

41. Robin and Rosie
42. Mark Curry
43. *Thomas the Tank Engine
    and Friends*
44. *Masters of the Universe*
45. Bananaman
46. *Byker Grove*
47. *The Amazing Adventures
    of Morph*
48. Jess
49. Peter Ustinov
50. Spotty

QUIZ 17

EVENTS

1. Sarah Ferguson
2. Shergar
3. 1985
4. Japan
5. The *Mary Rose*
6. Iran
7. Brighton
8. Galtieri
9. Alaska
10. Clapham Junction

11. 1988
12. San Francisco
13. Her son
14. Iraq
15. New Zealand
16. Spain
17. 1988
18. Leonid Breshnev
19. Solidarity
20. The Humber Bridge

21. Pioneer 10
22. Libya
23. Seven
24. 1983
25. 1980

26. Belgium
27. Michael Foot
28. HMS *York*
29. Lech Walesa
30. 1984

31. North Sea
32. Star Wars
33. Australia
34. Japan
35. Juventus
36. The Liberal Party
37. Mexico
38. Ivory
39. Conservatives
40. Francois Mitterand

41. United States
42. 1981
43. Harrods
44. Heinekein
45. Japan
46. Bradford City
47. British Telecom
48. Brinks Mat
49. Tottenham
50. Austria

QUIZ 18

TELEVISION

1. Pam
2. *Spitting Image*
3. *Bread*
4. *Allo, Allo*
5. *Yes, Minister*
6. Bono
7. *Crossroads*
8. Sylvester McCoy
9. *Neighbours*
10. Olivia

11. The Winchester Club
12. *Taxi*
13. *Brush Strokes*
14. Alan B'stard
15. Inspector Morse
16. Colby Co
17. Bobby, J. R and Gary Ewing and Ray Crebbs
18. *Albion Market*
19. Arnold Rimmer
20. Edward Woodward

21. *London's Burning*
22. Ruby Wax
23. Miss Ellie
24. The Ogdens
25. Moxy and Barry

26. *Knight Rider*
27. Tom Baker
28. *Just Good Friends*
29. *The Fall Guy*
30. Jackie Harris

31. *Red Dwarf*
32. *Tutti Frutti*
33. The Trotters (*Only Fools and Horses*)
34. *The Wonder Years*
35. Cilla Black
36. David McCallum
37. *Soap*
38. *The Young Ones*
39. Hale and Pace
40. *Manimal*

41. Jean-Luc Picard
42. Michael Buerk
43. Sir Humphrey Appleby
44. Michael Barrymore
45. *Family Fortunes*
46. 1988
47. Reginald Bosanquet
48. *The Dukes of Hazzard*
49. Frank Bough
50. 1980

MUSIC

1. Queen
2. Public Image Limited
3. Talking Heads
4. *Graceland*
5. Gloria Estefan
6. George Michael
7. 1984
8. Will Smith
9. Marillion
10. The Beat

11. The Flying Pickets
12. Paul Hardcastle
13. Bananarama
14. 'I Want to Break Free'
15. Fairground Attraction
16. The Cure
17. Metallica
18. 1984
19. Madness
20. Neil Diamond

21. Frankie Goes to Hollywood
22. Phil Collins
23. The Bee Gees
24. Eddie Van Halen

25. 'Spirit in the Sky'
26. The Communards
27. *October*
28. The Housemartins
29. 'Pump Up the Volume'
30. Bros

31. Pepsi and Shirlie
32. 'Nelly the Elephant'
33. John Wayne
34. The Jo Boxers
35. 1984
36. Bow Wow Wow
37. 'Enola Gay'
38. Visage
39. The Clash
40. Terence Trent D'Arby

41. Echo and the Bunnymen
42. 1980
43. *The Unforgettable Fire*
44. 1986
45. Matt, Luke and Craig
46. 1988
47. Cutting Crew
48. REM
49. Phil Oakey
50. 1987

QUIZ 20

FILMS AND FILM STARS

1. *When Harry Met Sally*
2. Robert De Niro
3. *The Blues Brothers*
4. Goldie Hawn
5. *E.T.*
6. *The Shining*
7. *The Killing Fields*
8. *Back to the Future*
9. *Pretty in Pink*
10. Derek Smalls

11. *Cocoon*
12. *Beetlejuice*
13. *Terms of Endearment*
14. *The Princess Bride*
15. *An American Werewolf in London*
16. *The Muppets take Manhattan*
17. Madonna
18. *Born on the Fourth of July*
19. Bud Fox
20. Paul Hogan

21. Molly Ringwald
22. Dan Ackroyd
23. Glenn Close
24. *An Officer and a Gentleman*

25. *Moonstruck*
26. Madison
27. *Raise the Titanic*
28. *Arthur*
29. *Gandhi*
30. *Chariots of Fire*

31. Gene Hackman
32. *Nine to Five*
33. Leslie Nielsen
34. *Spies Like Us, Airplane*
35. *Tootsie*
36. Jamie Lee Curtis
37. Beau and Jeff Bridges
38. *Trading Places*
39. Robert Redford
40. *Broadcast News*

41. B.B. King
42. Hulk Hogan and Mr T
43. *Staying Alive*
44. Debra Winger
45. Daryl Hannah
46. Bill Murray
47. *Crimes and Misdemeanours*
48. *Die Hard*
49. William Hurt
50. *Gremlins*

QUIZ 21

SCIENCE AND TECHNOLOGY

1. 1981
2. The compact disc
3. Halley's Comet
4. All early home computers
5. Liposuction
6. An underwater robot
7. Acid Rain
8. 1983
9. Post-it notes
10. Columbia

11. The hole in the ozone layer
12. Britain
13. 1984
14. A new form of carbon
15. MP3
16. 'Virtual reality'
17. Fuji
18. Disposable contact lenses
19. Prozac
20. Windows

21. 1986
22. Japan
23. Voyager 1

24. Centipede
25. Kodak disc film
26. DAT (Digital Audio Tape)
27. Uranus
28. Sony
29. *A Brief History of Time*
30. *National Geographic*

31. 1984
32. Travel into space
33. Antarctica
34. Mir
35. DNA
36. The Spectrum
37. An audio cassette tape
38. The *Titanic*
39. Eight
40. The World Wide Web

41. 25,000
42. Canada
43. 'Cyberspace'
44. Excel
45. The personal computer
46. The Lisa
47. CFCs
48. A mechanical heart
49. Compaq
50. A stealth fighter